# MAKING DOLLS' HOUSE FURNITURE

# MAKING DOLLS' HOUSE FURNITURE

## PATRICIA KING

Guild of Master Craftsman Publications

# Dedication

This book is dedicated to Jody, Rebecca, Leon and Oliver, who
all love making things.

A version of this book was first published in 1988 under the title
**Creating A Miniature World**. This revised and expanded edition
first published 1991 by Guild of Master Craftsman
Publications Ltd, Castle Place, 166 High Street, Lewes,
East Sussex BN7 1XU

First reprinted 1993
© Patricia King 1988, 1991
ISBN 0 946819 24 6
All rights reserved

Designed by Robert and Jean Wheeler Design Associates
Illustrations by Roderick King
Photographs by Richard Ball
Typeset By Central Southern Typesetters, Eastbourne

Printed and bound in Great Britain by
Hillman Printers (Frome) Ltd, Frome, Somerset.

# Acknowledgements

There are two Patricia Kings – the first is Pat King who can write and make things but not spell, punctuate or organize. The second is Patricia King the author who spells beautifully, punctuates impeccably and has everything organized with stunning efficiency. This is because various people, after having the vapours when they see the original draft, square up to the task and give generously of their expertise to help me appear professional.

So . . . my grateful thanks go to my long-suffering editor for her advice and apostrophes, and to my sister Claire for her support, help and patience in making her word processor translate writing that looked like someone's first attempt at knitting into a workmanlike script . . .

# Contents

# Foreword

A hobby only becomes a hobby when we put something of ourselves into it.

I have met scores of miniaturists who specialise in hand-crafting items in all kinds of materials – wood, clay, glass, copper, silver and so on – and one can build up a priceless collection of 'perfect' miniatures.

Pat King, however, has in this book put a new material firmly on the dolls' house map – 'rubbish'! When I first became involved in dolls' houses over a decade ago I found woodwork and needlecrafts difficult. I looked at the possible uses of throwaway packaging items but lacked Pat's imaginative ideas for making this amazing collection of very professional-looking miniatures. The financial outlay being minimal the end results are all the more remarkable.

Pat is a colourful figure – an enthusiast extraordinaire – and sitting in a class watching her almost literally pulling items out of a hat to make the Memsahib's commode from bracelet links, a shampoo nozzle etc., or Major Rhodeahead's exercise horse from a matchbox, half curler and so on, starts one's fingers itching.

This new, enlarged edition of her earlier book also includes a wonderful array of shops, including a pawnbroker, ironmonger and chemist, to lead you into even more exciting creations.

It is a privilege to share Pat's ideas and I guarantee that you too will soon become totally absorbed, looking at everyday items in such a way that you will be thinking . . . What can I use this for? Maybe you too have found a new hobby.

*Mary Churchill*
*Dorking, 1991*

# 1

# Introduction

*My friends and readers will know I like to improvise.
Buying things is all very well, but I find it more
challenging and rewarding to make things. After trying
all sorts of art and crafts forms, I settled down to the
hobby of making the furniture, effects and household
gadgets, not to mention people, for
a dolls' house set in 1900.*

Finding I lacked the skills to use tools that more sophisticated modellers depend upon, I turned to recycling on a small scale and roamed jumble sales, looking for likely makings. I found broken jewellery, buttons, finely turned chess pieces and the like that became the basis for wonderfully fussy Victorian pieces which I could never have made in the conventional way. An unexpected find of a bracelet with Indian motifs, which I turned into a panelled screen, became the missing 'link' in inventing the dolls' house family. Their characters quickly influenced the furnishings and their preferences pervaded the house – a peppery major, just back in 'Blighty' after service in India, his memsahib, and a staff of eccentric servants whose brief history I tell in the book.

Major Rhodeahead did not believe electricity would ever catch on and refused to have it in his house. This gave me a wonderful opportunity to research and make in miniature ingenious oil- and gas-powered Victorian gadgets and household objects, which I have used in the dolls' house and in shops. The rooms soon acquired that gleaming, ornate, cluttered look which was the fashion of the time.

A friend asked me to show the contents of my dolls' house at an annual crafts fair, so I made portable display boxes, furnished them, and took them along – not to sell, but to encourage people to make things for themselves. In the process I found there was a growing interest in scratch building so I began to write down how I made the furniture – and thus was born my first book: *Creating a Miniature World.*

It then seemed a natural progression to go on to making miniature shops. Partly through nostalgia and partly because my method of making things rejoices in elaborate twiddly-bits, I chose to stay in the Victorian era. My first shop was a present for a child. I bought a little hardboard farmhouse at an auction and set about making it into a toy baker's shop. I made bread, cakes and pastries from salt dough, using ice-cube holders as baskets. Even at five years old, the recipient sensed that the shop, made specially for her, was more individual than something bought, and treasured it. She has it still!!

As the baker's shop had been such fun to model, I went on to make a second shop for myself. This time there was an upstairs sitting/stock room, with a pot-bellied stove, a gas stove, armchair, a cat sleeping on the hot bread, and shelves of bread and cakes, all hugger-mugger as they used to be before hygiene laws came in. This shop opened at the back, so the wares could be arranged on the shelves.

Friends, who know I use all sorts of bits, sometimes give me things, and that's how I became the owner of a set of miniature tools – hammer, pliers, scissors and the like, which asked to be made into something. As a result the ironmonger's was born, with the fussy forecourt display ironmongers used to have.

My chemist came about in another way. I had to have a tetanus injection and was allowed to keep the glass ampoule which contained the vaccine. A friend who worked for a vet saved me similar ampoules and I soon had a collection of scale glass jars. It was then just a question of whether I should use them in a sweetshop or a chemist's. The chemist's won, but I hope to make a sweetshop in the future.

The pawnbroker's started with a shop kit. I had amassed quite a few makes from the first dolls' house and it seemed a good idea to put spares into a shop. Miniature antiques shops have been done before, so a pawnshop seemed a good alternative. My husband suggested Arthur Tick as the name of the proprietor and I was ready to start.

Making antique dolls' house furniture out of jumble sale junk is a fascinating and inexpensive hobby. It satisfies a number of my interests – I love jumble sales, antiques and dolls' houses; I like to own beautiful things, but I cannot afford them, so I make them in miniature. I go about my creations in one of two ways: either a jumble sale find suggests a purpose it might be put to, or I decide I want to make a certain piece of furniture and look for the wherewithal to make it. I am not an expert at turning, soldering or woodwork, so I have to find substitutes, keep tools down to a minimum, and my workshop is the kitchen table.

If like me you enjoy improvising, here are descriptions of how I go about making my dolls' house, shops and the contents. Of course you may do it differently, but I hope this book will start you off.

Good luck in your enterprise and happy modelling!

# 2

# The Rhodeahead Family

*Once upon a time, 2 Chipsand Place WC2 served as the town residence of the Rhodeahead family. There was Major Rufus Rhodeahead, formerly of India, where he served in the 23rd Veriipaur Lancers, his Memsahib, Elaine (née Closure) and the usual retinue of servants.*

## Major Rhodeahead

Born in 1845, the second son of E. C. Rhodeahead Bart., Rufus (Ruff) was destined for the army. Expelled from Harrow (where the desk he carved with his initials is now proudly displayed) he attended Eton for the Michaelmas term, and was asked to leave Sandhurst after the unfortunate incident of the four roast ducks.

At the age of 22 he took a private passage to India where he was notorious for his progress on the polo field and with the ladies. He received a Viceroy's commission in the 23rd Veriipaur Lancers, serving in India between 1867 and 1895, where he met and married the Mem. Their son, Wally, was born in 1871. He distinguished himself at the siege of Aquabad, earning himself the name of Rabid Rhodeahead. The Major retired to Chipsand Place in 1895, arriving in Blighty* in time for the grouse season.

A good representation of the Major can be found on page 77.

## The Mem

Much has been written about the Mem. Born in 1851 in India into a military family, the name of the former Elaine Closure was constantly in the fashion and society magazines. She was known for her flaming red hair, fine figure and good seat, and notorious for the incident when she appeared at a polo match wearing bloomers and sitting astride the horse instead of side-saddle, as becoming to a brigadier's daughter. It is said that only the Viceroy's prompt offering of his hand to help her alight avoided a riot.

Since her husband's retirement to Blighty, the Mem has taken to her bed suffering (she says) from recurring bouts of malaria, though you may notice among the medications on her bedside table a large bottle of gin. She is seen on page 33 with a glass of port in her hand.

## Addington the Butler

Addington is always referred to as the 'new' butler, having succeeded his father some thirty years ago. He is rather eccentric but, in the absence of the Mem, holds the house together and rules it with a rod of iron. He is allowed to wear slippers as he suffers dreadfully with his feet. It has been whispered that his complaint is gout, brought on by a predilection for the Major's port. Certainly I have found him lying full length many times, when I have left him standing. I have been forced to lock the liquor cupboard, and now cook wears the key hanging from her belt! Major Rhodeahead, however, will not entertain for a moment the idea that Addington is suffering from gout, as that malady can only be suffered by the upper classes. He fears his butler is giving himself airs, and says firmly that his discomfort is due at best to fallen arches.

*Blighty: Brit. slang (used esp. by troops serving abroad) 1. England. 2. Home. [from Hindi *bilayati* foreign land] – an expression very much 'of the people'. PK.

# Mrs Mentry the Cook

Mrs Mentry, the cook, dominates the lower ground floor
including, of course, the kitchen and everything that goes on in it.
The title 'Mrs' is honorary, for she is in fact unmarried, but she has
an 'understanding' with Arthur Crown the part-time gardener,
who is a great admirer of her cooking. Even Arthur addresses her
as Mrs Mentry, though the butler, being a social equal, is allowed
to address her as Ella, her Christian name. Though a stickler
for perfection, Mrs Mentry keeps a motherly eye on the skivvy,
Watson, who she is training to be a cook's help.

# Penge the Sewing Lady

Penge is not a live-in member of the staff. She comes in twice a
week to do sewing and a little light 'goffering'. She knew the
Memsahib in the old days and is tolerated for this reason. She used
to be the Mem's dressmaker when the Mem was known to be a
leader of fashion, but now the Mem never gets up and does not,
therefore, require any gowns. This is just as well as Penge cannot
see more than an inch beyond her nose. Neither she nor the Mem
have noticed that the dress form, which was once used to fit the
Mem's dresses, no longer bears any resemblance to the plump
lady in the bed. Penge rarely makes anything nowadays. She and
the Mem drink gin and quarrel and remember the good old days.

# Polly Esther the Nanny

Seen here Holding the Hon. Horatio Snott (the Rhodeaheads' only
grandson), Miss Esther is new to the house. She succeeded Nanny
Blog, who had been with the Rhodeaheads some 30 years, and was
given a small pension, which allows her to live in Norfolk.

Though I find Miss Esther of an amiable disposition, I am a
little worried about her habit of wearing provocative striped
stockings under her uniform.

# Hetty Kate and the Hon. Horatio Snott

The grandchildren are aged six years and six months respectively.
They have lived at Chipsand Place ever since they lost both parents
on a brave but ill-fated expedition to take photographs of the
secret dance of the little-known Impetigo Head Hunters. Eight
native bearers were also lost, and the National Geographical
Society, which sponsored the venture, reported the expedition in a
special issue which came out in May and had black edges to the
cover. The Hon. Horatio Snott is, of course, heir to the title and
will in time inherit the half-castle in Scotland and the fine
collection of emu eggs.

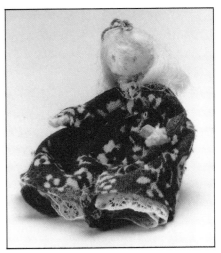

# 3

# Basic Boxes

*When you come down to it, each room setting or shop is a box, a dolls' house being a series of boxes. So I have chosen to present this book as a collection of individual boxes, each with its contents, and in the case of shops their exteriors as well.*

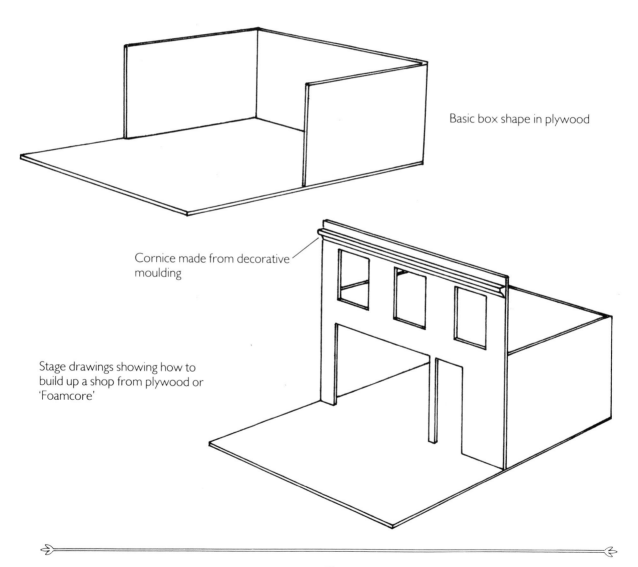

Basic box shape in plywood

Cornice made from decorative moulding

Stage drawings showing how to build up a shop from plywood or 'Foamcore'

# Ideas for a Shop

I am no carpenter! If I try to saw a straight line, I find in no time that my saw is marooned half-way through its journey, starts to squeal, and someone has to rescue both it and me. So I prefer *furnishing* rooms and shops rather than making them. However, the appearance of a ready made kit may need adapting and I use various materials to serve my purpose.

If you share my experience of fighting a losing battle with tools, some of my ideas may also help you to make basic buildings, although I must stress that these are guidelines only, not explicit instructions.

Start by finding a box large enough to house your interior – about 13″ × 10½″ × 9″ is a useful size. If you can't find anything suitable, jot down the dimensions you want and visit the nearest DIY shop; they will advise you on what materials you need and cut the pieces to size. I find that 6mm plywood is a good choice.

You will need a back piece and two matching sides, also in the case of a shop a base which can be extended forward to allow for a pavement display. Make the lid of your box from clear plastic sheeting, to allow maximum light inside. This sheeting can be scored and then cracked along the score-line, so bypassing the use of the dreaded saw. The front should rise above the box top to hide the box. Trim with a cornice made from decorative moulding. Use a fretsaw to cut out door and window spaces, or get someone to do it for you! My finished façades lift off the base they rest on, and are held to the box by bar magnets.

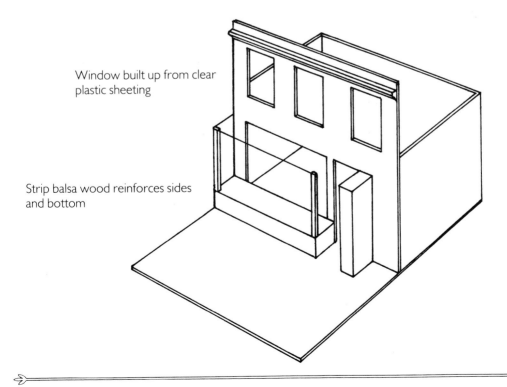

Window built up from clear plastic sheeting

Strip balsa wood reinforces sides and bottom

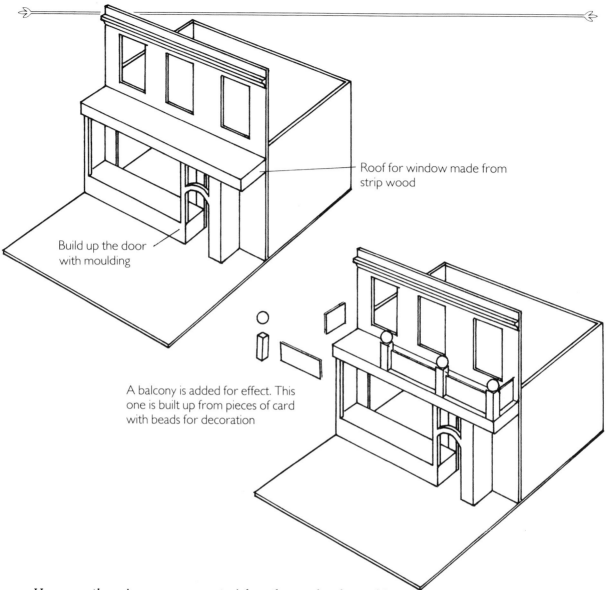

Roof for window made from
strip wood

Build up the door
with moulding

A balcony is added for effect. This
one is built up from pieces of card
with beads for decoration

However, there is now a new material on the market for making
settings and I recommend it highly. An excellent alternative to
plywood, it is called Foamcore and is a laminate of two sheets of
card with polystyrene sandwiched between. Light but firm, it cuts
cleanly with a craft knife and doesn't warp, with the added
advantage that you can pin parts together using dressmaking pins
– allowing you to adjust the fit before gluing in place. Also it takes
glue and paint well. It is available in large sheets, 20″ × 30″, and
in 2mm and 5mm thicknesses, in art shops.

Build up the shop window from two sides and a front made of
clear plastic sheeting, reinforced at the sides and below with strip
wood. Adhesive mouldings, available at DIY shops, are decorative
and useful for door arches and pilasters.

There are many, many variations on this basic model, some of
which are seen later in the book. Using the simple materials
described, you can make your shop just as you like.

# Simple Room Setting

Whether you display your treasured dolls' house furniture in a box, shelf or deep picture frame, it is quite easy to make that space look like a room. All my backgrounds are made in this way and it gives me maximum flexibility for showing and photographing the miniature furniture and effects. It gives shape to the room and creates recesses and a chimney-breast, to which you can add a fireplace.

## Materials

*Cardboard*
*Wrapping paper (small pattern)*

## Method

1 Cut the cardboard to the height of your box and score and bend it to the shape shown, creating side walls, fireplaces and recesses at either side of the fireplace.
2 Paper the walls with gift-wrap paper to give a really plausible look to the room.

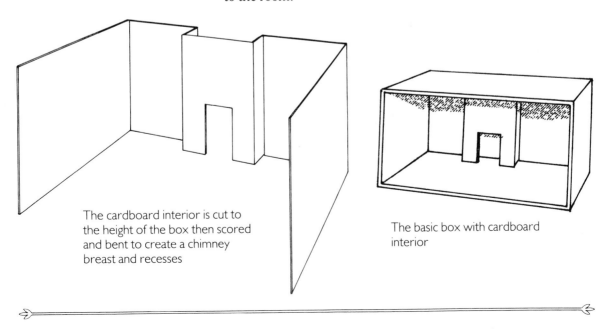

The cardboard interior is cut to the height of the box then scored and bent to create a chimney breast and recesses

The basic box with cardboard interior

# Fireplaces

**Materials**

*Stiff card*
*Small square fancy picture frame*
*Curved frame*
*Balsa wood*
*Ornate buckle or brooch*

Fireplaces, more than any other feature, set the period and style of your dolls' house. Luckily they are rarely built in, so the way is clear for you to put in your own individually made ones. Even if you do not possess a dolls' house, and display your furniture on a shelf or in a box, you can enhance the scene and set the tone by adding a fireplace. I usually start by making a chimney breast and then building up the fireplace.

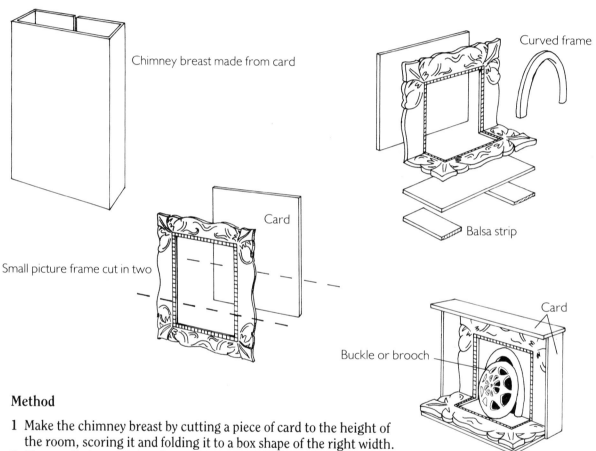

Chimney breast made from card

Curved frame

Card

Balsa strip

Small picture frame cut in two

Buckle or brooch

Card

## Method

1 Make the chimney breast by cutting a piece of card to the height of the room, scoring it and folding it to a box shape of the right width.
2 The small picture frame forms the surround and hearth when cut in two as shown.
3 Cut two pieces of card to fit the two halves of the frame.
4 The arch of the fireplace is made by using a curved frame of some kind, e.g. a doll's mirror with the bottom cut off.
5 Stick the arch on to the card backing of the fireplace, then draw round the inside of the curve and cut out the arch shape.
6 Raise the card inside the hearth part of the frame on strips of balsa wood to form a step, and stick to the back of the frame.
7 The mantelpiece and sides can be built up using strips of card or balsa.
8 Prop a fussy buckle in front of the hole to make a fireguard (and to save making the inside of the grate!).

# THE HOUSE

# 4

# Trophy Room

*The Trophy Room is the Major's lair. Here, surrounded by mementoes of past glories, he can reminisce about his days in India. The Trophy Room is very masculine and completely sacrosanct, apart from the occasional shuffling intrusion by Addington.*

# Desk

## Materials

*Box top*
*Stiff card*
*Light card*
*Metal bead caps*
*Beads*

This desk was tailor-made to fit a shaped box top that I found in a jumble sale.

### Method

1 Make the body of the desk from stiff card, scoring and bending to achieve the required shape.
2 Face the front with light card, then cut out and superimpose the dummy drawers.
3 Stick the box top on to the body of the desk.
4 Spray the desk brown and drag a brush through the paint just before it dries to give the walnut effect.
5 The handles are metal bead caps with beads on top, threaded on to pins.

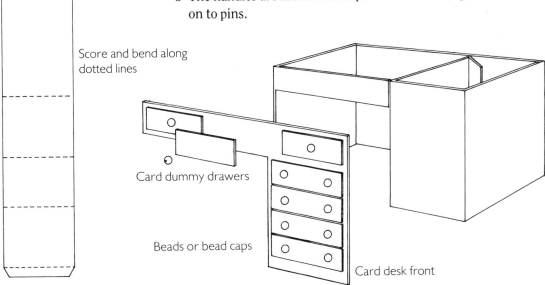

Score and bend along dotted lines

Card dummy drawers

Beads or bead caps

Card desk front

# Desk-top Accessories

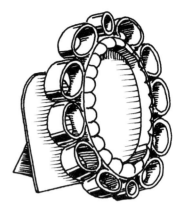

*Quill pen in ink stand*
Simply trim a likely feather and
glue it into a bead.

*Blotter (curved)*
Cut the balsa wood to shape and
top with a piece of card, bead cap
and bead.

*Portrait of Mem*
Mount a suitable photo in an
earring from which the stone has
been removed. Back with a card
stand.

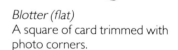

*Pencils in jar*
Sharpened lengths of cocktail
stick in a bead cap with washer
added as base.

*Ruler*
Tiny sliver of card or balsa.

*Blotter (flat)*
A square of card trimmed with
photo corners.

*Military trophy*
A propped-up badge.

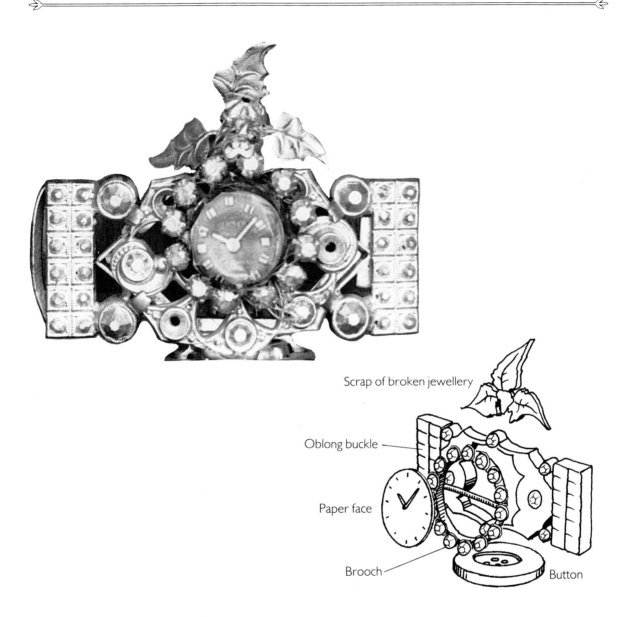

Scrap of broken jewellery

Oblong buckle

Paper face

Brooch

Button

# Presentation Clock

The Presentation Clock was given to Major Rhodeahead when he left the 23rd Veriipaur Lancers. It is in faultless bad taste and now has pride of place on the mantelpiece in the Trophy Room. For other clocks, see pages 134–5.

**Materials**

*Oblong filigree and diamanté buckle*
*Fancy brass button*
*Diamanté brooch, minus central stone*
*Clock face cut from a catalogue*
*Various ornamental odds and ends*

### Method

The brooch, minus central stone, encloses the clock face, and is mounted on the oblong buckle. The fancy brass button forms the base, and odd bits of decoration can be added to the top.

**Materials**

*Buckles*
*Earrings*
*Brooches*
*Pendants*
*Pictures of suitable subjects*

# Picture, Map and Document Framing

Major Rhodeahead has two great passions in life – his service in the Indian Army and pretty girls. His pictures reflect his interest in both! At first his trophy room only had respectable pictures – a tiger shoot, a portrait of Queen Victoria and various photographs of posed regimental groups. But as the Mem took more and more to her bed, it became obvious that she never visited the trophy room, and a change began to take place. A pipe rack appeared, then photos of the beauties of the day, wearing large hats and what look curiously like thermal vests to our eyes, provocatively posed, and displayed above his desk.

Finding photos, maps and documents which reflected the Major's preoccupation was not too hard, but they were all much too large, generally postcard size! At first I looked for the right-sized people in the background of larger subjects, but soon found that too limiting. The problem was solved by taking all the postcard-sized pictures to a photocopying service, asking them to be reduced by half, and then reducing the resulting half-sized photocopy to half-size, and so on through about six reductions, until I bore away one A4 sheet of photocopy paper on which were printed 25 stamp-sized photos. These were surprisingly clear, and I was then able to back the whole sheet with thin card and cut out and mount each individual picture.

### Method

1 Remove central stones from earrings, brooches, pendants, etc.
2 Reduce pictures by photocopying smaller and smaller.
3 Fix tiny pictures to backs of frames.

Small brooch

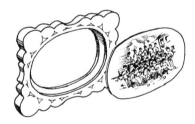

Brooch with stone removed

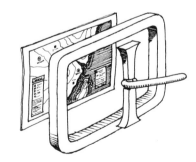

Buckle with centre bar removed

# Mounted Trophies

While I am sure it is quite indefensible to thus mutilate a plastic zoo animal, you must admit it gives authenticity to a Victorian study or hall! A nice touch is a tiny plate underneath cut from a square of tin foil.

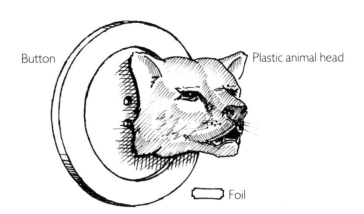

Button     Plastic animal head     Foil

### Method

1 Cut the head off the plastic animal.
2 Mount it on the button.
3 Make a tiny plaque from tin foil.

### Materials

*Plastic zoo animals*
*Fancy button*
*Foil*

# Tiger Skin Rug

Major Rhodeahead has probably told you in great detail the story of how he single-handedly sought out and shot the tiger that had terrorized the whole of the district. He has certainly told everyone else, and if you have been spared the details I won't be the one to spoil a good tale. You can see for yourself the one bullet hole in the tiger's forehead. The rug has pride of place in front of the fireplace.

### Materials

*Beige felt*
*Modelling dough (I used Barbola paste)*
*Thin card*
*Plastic zoo tiger (optional)*
*Green beads*

## Method

1  Either model a tiger's head, or use the plastic animal's head.
2  Copy the shape on this page and cut from the felt.
3  Pad the paws with modelling dough.
4  Stick on a backing of thin card.
5  Bring the felt to a point to blend the head into the neck.
6  Add the stripes with a felt pen.
7  Stick the green beads on for eyes
   if the head is modelled.

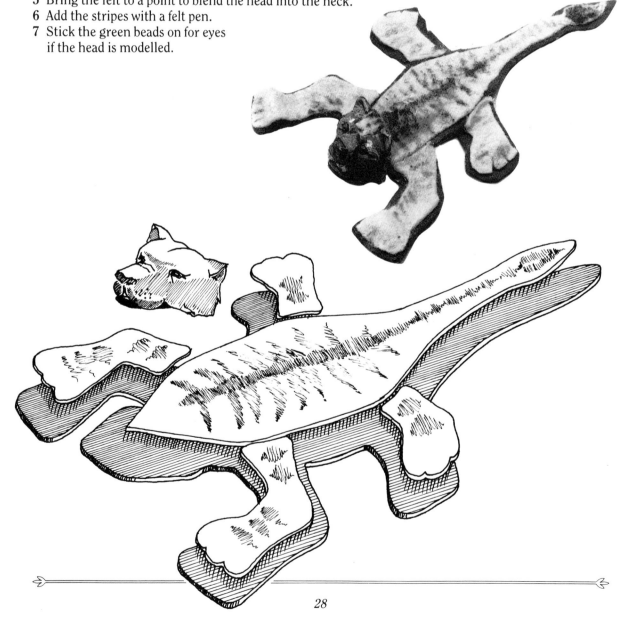

# Highland Shield and Swords

You may be lucky enough to find ready-made small swords. The ones in the photograph came in a 'Present from Toledo'! If you aren't so fortunate, why not use 'cocktail swords'. The bear and car on either side of the presentation clock (see page 25) are from a charm bracelet, each mounted on a button.

## Materials

*Metal brooch*
*'Cocktail swords' (or other*
*small swords)*
*Metallic car spray paint*

## Method

1 Spray 'swords' with paint to give metallic finish.
2 Lace them through the brooch.
3 An embossed centre piece finishes the effect.

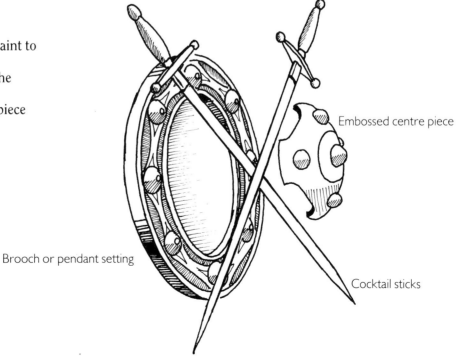

Embossed centre piece

Brooch or pendant setting

Cocktail sticks

# Hanging Oil Lamp

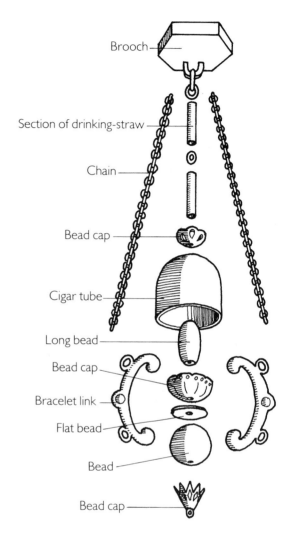

Brooch

Section of drinking-straw

Chain

Bead cap

Cigar tube

Long bead

Bead cap

Bracelet link

Flat bead

Bead

Bead cap

## Method

1 The bottom piece cut from the cigar tube forms the dome of the lamp.
2 Put the elongated bead inside the dome, with a bead cap beneath and bead under that.
3 On either side of the bead, glue the two halves of the bracelet link.
4 The piece of drinking-straw, with a bead cap underneath, forms the tube of the lamp, and can be made in sections with extra links and beads.
5 Suspend the lamp from the ceiling with fine chains attached to the pieces of bracelet link.
6 A ceiling rose can be made from a brooch, and the lamp hung from that.

## Materials

*Plastic cigar tube*
*Bracelet link*
*Beads*
*Bead caps*
*Transparent drinking-straw*
*Chain*
*Brooch*

# Books

Books, in sets or single volumes, help to make a room look
lived in.

## Materials

### Single Books
*Balsa wood strip*
*Leather or leatherette*
  *(e.g. from an old diary)*
*Cotton*

### Sets of Books
*Polystyrene container*
*Paint and varnish*

## Method

### Single Books
1 Cut a length of leather (or leatherette) long enough for several books.
2 Cut a length from the balsa strip to form the body of the books.
3 Score the leather and wrap around three sides of the balsa strip.
4 Cut into individual books.
5 Band the spine with the cotton.

### Sets of Books
1 Cut a strip from the polystyrene.
2 Score it heavily vertically to represent individual volumes.
3 Score across the row at intervals to represent binding ribs.
4 Paint and varnish – but do not spray or it will melt!

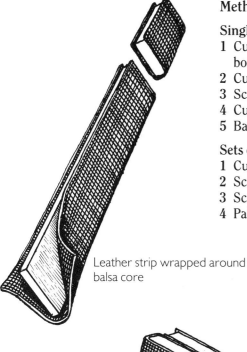

Leather strip wrapped around
balsa core

Individual books cut from strip

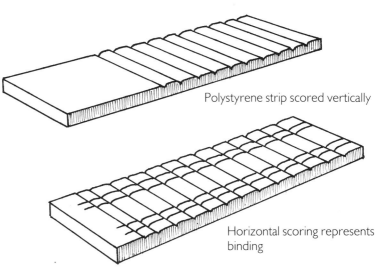

Polystyrene strip scored vertically

Horizontal scoring represents
binding

# Carriage Lamps

A handsome pair of carriage lamps graces the chimney breast of the trophy room, and they are so easy to make!

## Materials

*Piece of old transparent Biro barrel*
*Bead caps*
*Dress-studs*
*Tiny gold bead*
*Piece of foil, or bent link, or metal button with looped shaft*

## Method

1 Construct the lamps in the order shown in the exploded drawing: tiny bead, bead cap, Biro barrel, bead cap, dress-stud.
2 Mount on the wall either using the strip of foil, the bent link, or the button with its shaft outwards, and the stem of the dress-stud slotted through.

Small bead —— ○

Bead cap ——

Section of clear ballpoint pen case ——

Bead cap ——

Dress-stud ——

Button with metal shank ——

The kitchen, complete with servants' bells and fresh-baked bread.

All the comforts of home are found in the sitting room.

The imposing billiard room.

Toys help to create a colourful nursery.

The Mem, with breakfast tray and glass of gin!

*Below left* The exercise horse looks very dusty – unlike the commode.

Addington shuffles through the hall, past traditional armour and grandfather clock.

The dining room is darkly panelled and features a fine fireplace.

Penge in the surroundings of her little sewing room.

*Below right* The Rhodeahead household gathered in the dining room.

*Below* The scullery, with primitive labour-saving devices.

The bathroom – with bath occupied!

The Major's lair, with mementoes of past glories.

# Mem's Bedroom

*Having virtually taken up permanent residence in her bedroom, the Mem insists on a very feminine and lady-like atmosphere, hence the clutter of bottles and jars and the fussy confusion of furniture.*

# Dressing Table

## Method

1  Make the four legs from strips of balsa.
2  Mount the matchbox on the legs and use the bracelet links for front and side panels.
3  Make four more smaller legs to support the raised part, which can either be a piece of balsa cut to size, or card scored and bent to make a box shape.
4  Before adding mats, ornaments and mirror, spray the whole thing brown.
5  The mirror is an elaborate brooch with the reflective foil set in for glass. It is supported by two more legs, with ornamental odds and ends to conceal joins.
6  Pieces of doyley form the mats.
7  Finish off with bottles (see opposite), candlesticks (see page 46), etc.

### Materials

*Swan Vestas matchbox*
*Balsa wood strip*
*Links from metal filigree*
  *bracelet*
*Brooch setting*
*Reflective metal e.g. from*
  *sealing foil of coffee*
  *container*
*Pieces of paper doyley*

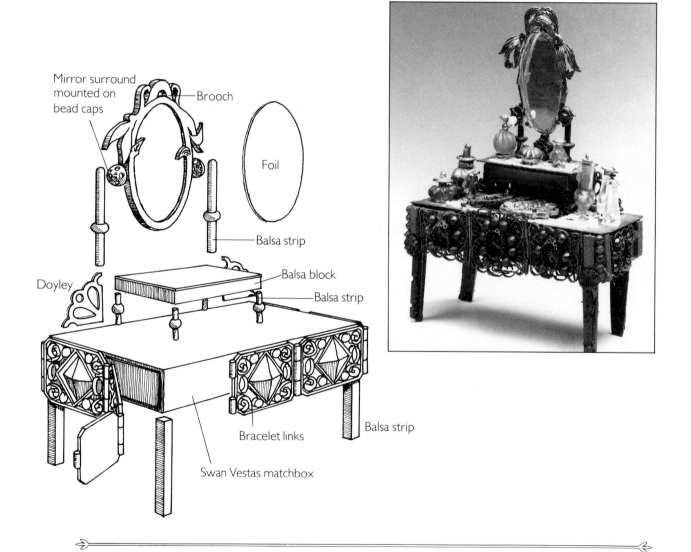

Mirror surround mounted on bead caps

Brooch

Foil

Balsa strip

Doyley

Balsa block

Balsa strip

Bracelet links

Balsa strip

Swan Vestas matchbox

# Glass Ornaments and Objects

Grace the tables, shelves and kitchen cupboard of your dolls' house with these very plausible-looking 'glass' ornaments. There are many combinations of the materials below to experiment with.

## Method

1 Sections can be cut from clear plastic 'Toni' curlers and topped with beads to make scent bottles.
2 Use glass or plastic buttons or beads, or small glass drawer handles, topped with bead caps, and tiny beads for handles.

## Materials

*Glass or plastic buttons*
*Glass or plastic beads*
*Metal bead caps*
*'Toni' curlers*
*Dress-studs*
*Washers*

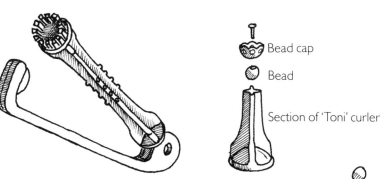

Bead cap

Bead

Section of 'Toni' curler

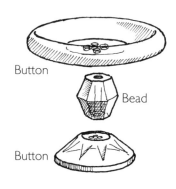

Button

Bead

Button

Bead cap

Faceted bead

Washer

Button

Square bead

Bead cap

Bead

Button

Clear button

Dress-stud

# Breakfast Tray

I paid 5p for the brooch in a jumble sale. 'Just the thing,' I thought, as I enthusiastically wrenched the pin off the back to make it into a tray. I found a link that would make carrying handles for it, glued them on so that they would never come off and used a tiny button for a plate, etc. When it was finished, I showed the result to my daughter with pride. She nearly had a fit! 'That brooch,' she wailed weakly, 'was Art Nouveau and worth at least £35!' Well, it isn't now.

**Materials**

*Brooch*
*Links from chain*
*Buttons*
*Necklace fastener*
*Beads*
*Screw-type earring*
*Part of cake-candle-holder*

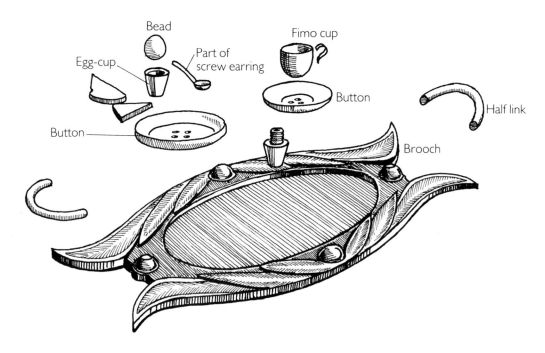

**Method**

**Tray**
See above!

**Cup**
See Crockery, page 90. The pattern round the rim is drawn with felt-tip pen.

**Egg Cup and Salt Cellar**
These are the two halves of a necklace fastener, with a bead for the egg.

**Spoon**
The screw-type earring is straightened out and the screw removed.

# Commode

The Mem has taken to her bed suffering, she claims, from recurring bouts of malaria, which she alleviates with large quantities of gin – purely medicinally of course! As she rarely leaves her bed it was quite urgent that I made a commode and the Mem was much relieved when it was completed. This piece is one of my favourites and actually has a hinged lid which lifts to reveal 'my lady's chamber'.

## Method

1  Cut the card and fold it to make a box for the chair base, making a square cut-out in the front panel to house your small bracelet link.
2  Glue the link into the cut-out shape and make up the box.
3  The bugle bead forms the hinge and the paper fastener the handle on the front panel.
4  From the card cut a seat shape with a hole in it to frame the shampoo nozzle. Glue this in place to complete your box seat.
5  Cut a shape to fit the seat to make the lid. Attach the hinge to it.
6  Cut a chair back from the card to suit your box base, removing a square shape to make a hole to frame the larger rectangular link.
7  Fix the link in position behind the frame and glue the back to the base of the chair.
8  Reinforce the back with two balsa uprights, each topped with a bead.
9  Decorate the top of the chair back with the necklace clasp.
10  Use cellulose paint to spray the commode and lid brown before you attach the lid to the base. (Put cork in the shampoo nozzle to stop it being coloured while spraying.)
11  Glue the hinge in place so that the lid can be raised and lowered.
12  Use the two halves of the chain link to make arms on either side of the lid.

## Materials

*Stiff card*
*Two rectangular bracelet links –*
*    one large, one small*
*A large oval chain link cut in half*
*Shampoo nozzle*
*Necklace clasp*
*Tiny hinge*
*A bugle bead*
*Two small flat beads*
*Brass paper fastener*

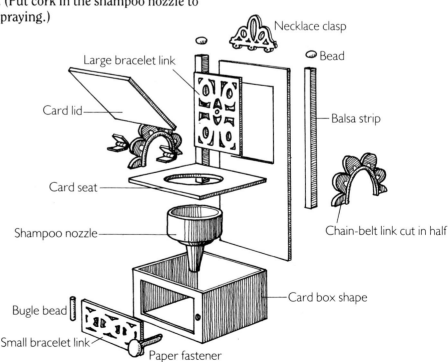

Necklace clasp

Large bracelet link

Bead

Card lid

Balsa strip

Card seat

Chain-belt link cut in half

Shampoo nozzle

Bugle bead

Card box shape

Small bracelet link

Paper fastener

# 6

# Sitting Room

*The Sitting Room is a wonderful place to furnish. You can fill it with over-stuffed chairs, decorative little tables, shiny lamps and so on. Many of the objects from The Pawnbroker could be swapped with those already in this room. The effect should be as cluttered and elaborate as possible.*

# Armchairs or Sofa

The size or shape can be varied to make a winged chair or couch.

## Materials

*Balsa wood, ¼" thick*
*Thin card*
*Cotton wadding*
*Velvet or other fine material*
*Lampshade gimp*

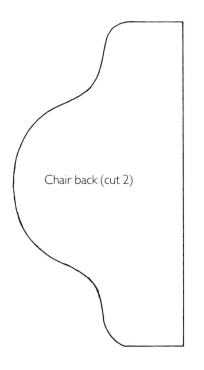

Chair back (cut 2)

### Method

1  Cut two backs and one seat bottom from the card.
2  Cut another seat bottom from the balsa wood.
3  Pad the balsa wood base and one of the card backs with the wadding.
4  Cover these padded parts and the other card back with the velvet or other material, turning over the raw edges as shown in the diagram.
5  Stick the card base to the balsa base so that no raw edges show.
6  Bend the padded back round the seat and glue into place – the raw edges will show at the back and sides.
7  Glue the unpadded, covered back to the other one, thus hiding all the raw edges.
8  Trim with the gimp.

General construction

Chair seat

Fabric
Padding
Card

Fabric
Padding
Balsa
Card

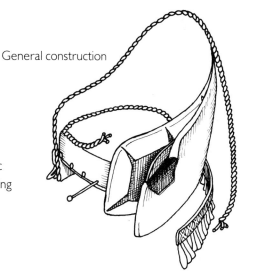

# Bookcase

This piece was made in card in box form. 'How can I make a set of see-through doors all to match?' I asked myself. The answer was to use the links of a metal bracelet. I cut out all the doorways and inserted see-through plastic panels, which I then framed with the links! The books in the bottom row are made individually (see Trophy Room, page 31). The top row are magazine photos of books.

**Materials**

*Card*
*Four identical bracelet links*
*Beads*
*Bead caps*
*Plastic sheet*

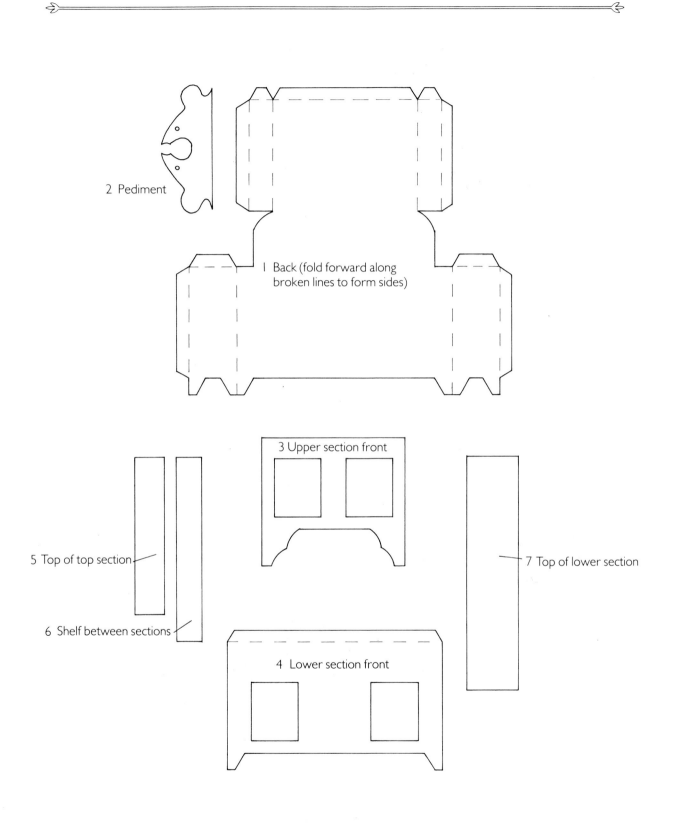

2 Pediment

1 Back (fold forward along broken lines to form sides)

3 Upper section front

5 Top of top section

6 Shelf between sections

7 Top of lower section

4 Lower section front

## Method

1 Cut all the pieces for the body of the bookcase from card, scoring and bending as shown.
2 Cut out the four main doors and 'glaze' them with plastic sheet.
3 Frame these doors with the links, and use either tiny beads or bead caps as handles.
4 Build up the drawers and centre panels using pieces of card, and trim with beads and bead caps.
5 The remaining oblong shapes are shelves, which from widest at the bottom to narrowest at the top, are fixed in place.

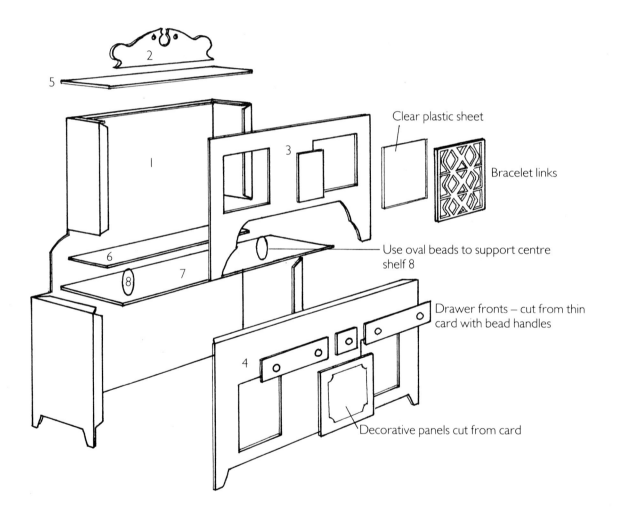

Clear plastic sheet

Bracelet links

Use oval beads to support centre shelf 8

Drawer fronts – cut from thin card with bead handles

Decorative panels cut from card

# Overmantel and Fireplace

## Materials

*Stiff card or balsa wood*
*Narrow lampshade gimp*
*Mirror (approx. 5cm × 5cm)*
*Necklace clasp*
*Strings of beads*

Any overmantel you make really becomes an elaborate frame for a mirror, so first find a small handbag mirror that is in scale with your fireplace, and then adapt my pattern accordingly. Try to leave sticking the mirror in place until you have made up as much of the frame as you can, then you can spray the frame. Of course, the shelves that actually cross the mirror must be left till last, but it helps if most of the overmantel is spray-painted in advance.

## Method

1 The overmantel basic backing shape is made from either stiff card or balsa.
2 Cut four each of the short and long curved side pieces, one long shelf, two short shelves, two medium shelves, one shelf of a length to go above the two arches, and two pieces as sides to this top layer. A leather punch is an effective way of stamping out the sharp curves on the side supports.
3 Build up the front of the overmantel as shown.
4 Use lampshade braid to decorate the mantelpiece.
5 Rows of beads are also used for decoration as shown. These are best sprayed brown before being positioned.
6 The necklace clasp decorates the pediment.
7 Various other ornamental devices can be used, such as scrolls of paper and beads, to finish off the effect.

General layout showing position of

1 Short uprights (×4)
2 Long uprights (×4)
3 Short shelves (×2)
4 Long shelves (×2)
5 Mirror

Construction

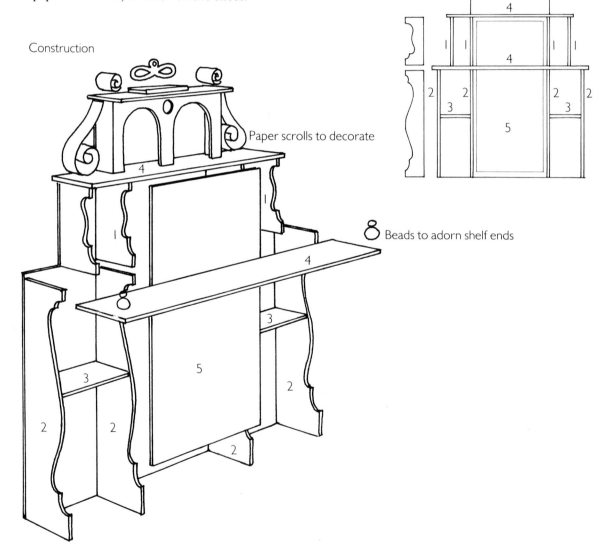

Paper scrolls to decorate

Beads to adorn shelf ends

## Materials

### Tables
*Buckle, brooch or button*
*Square piece of leather*
*Bead, bead cap or button*
*Lipstick case, chess piece or*
    *scent-bottle top*

### Candlestick
*Drawing pin*
*Belt-hole liner*
*Bead cap*
*Paper*
*Sewing cotton*

# Occasional Tables

A table could start with a plastic buckle that looks like figured walnut and a base made from a scent-bottle top. Brooches and buttons can also be used for the tops, and chess pieces or lipstick cases for the bases. Fancy buttons can replace beads.

## Method

### Tables
1  If using a brooch for the table top, remove the stone.
2  Fill the hole in the brooch or buckle, or cover the surface of the button, with a piece of leather.
3  Add the bead, bead cap or button 'spacer'.
4  The lipstick case, scent-bottle top or chess piece becomes the base of the table.

### Candlesticks
1  The drawing pin topped with the belt-hole liner, then the bead cap, forms the candlestick.
2  Make the candle from the rolled-up paper with the sewing cotton threaded through.

Cotton
Paper
Bead cap
Belt-hole liner
Drawing pin
Large button
Small button

Part of chess piece

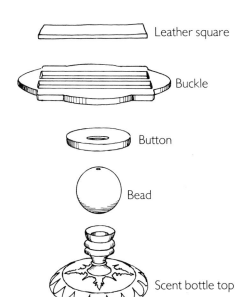

Leather square
Buckle
Button
Bead
Scent bottle top

# Candlesticks

I couldn't believe my luck when I saw an evening dress trimmed with plastic bells in a jumble sale. I knew as soon as I saw them that they would make wonderful gas lamps (see Ceiling Lights, page 97). They have stood me in good stead ever since. Just in case you find some, here is how they can also make candlesticks. There are many variations of this sequence, see page 49 for another suggestion.

## Method

1 Follow the diagram for the sequence of bell, bead cap, bead, bead cap, bead, diamond-shaped bead, bead cap, glass button.
2 Thread in this order on to the needle, gluing them into place. This will stop them getting out of line.

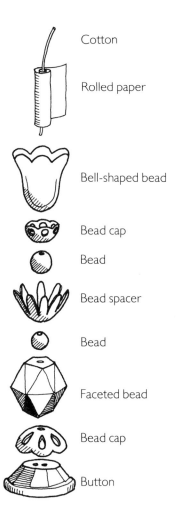

Cotton

Rolled paper

Bell-shaped bead

Bead cap

Bead

Bead spacer

Bead

Faceted bead

Bead cap

Button

## Materials

*Bell-shaped bead*
*Bead caps*
*Bead spacers*
*Beads*
*Glass button*
*Long needle*

# Table Lamps

There are many combinations of materials from which to make lamps. A lovely filigree earring with the stone removed, a large pearl bead, or a brilliant faceted bead can form the basis for all kinds of variations. Some of the most useful materials are listed below.

### Method

In order to line up the parts, thread them on to a needle, then glue them into place and to each other.

### Materials

*Biro refill tubes*
*Earring settings and screws*
*Pearl beads*
*Diamond beads*
*Bugle beads*
*Metal bead caps of all sizes*
*Cylindrical spacers*
*Buttons, plain and fancy*
*All kinds of other beads!*

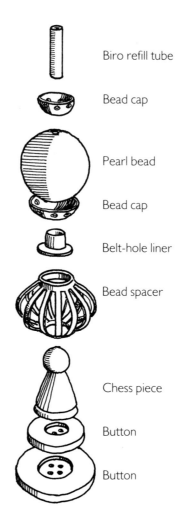

Biro refill tube

Bead cap

Pearl bead

Bead cap

Belt-hole liner

Bead spacer

Chess piece

Button

Button

# Piano

I used 'Toni' hair curlers for legs and pieces of necklace clasp for the music stand.

## Materials

*Shiny card*
*Balsa or stiff card*
*Toni hair curlers*
*Necklace clasp*
*Pieces of filigree bracelet link*
*00 gauge model railway fence*
*Bead cap*
*Cotton*
*Fine paper*
*Brown cellulose car spray paint*

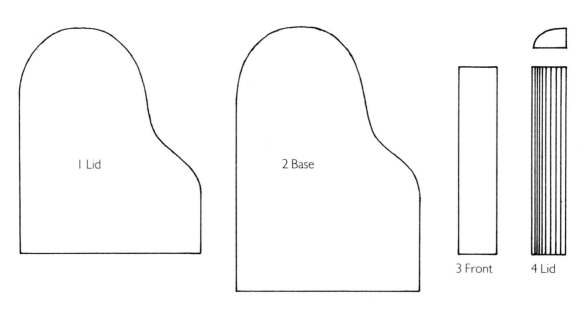

1 Lid

2 Base

3 Front

4 Lid

5 Side piece

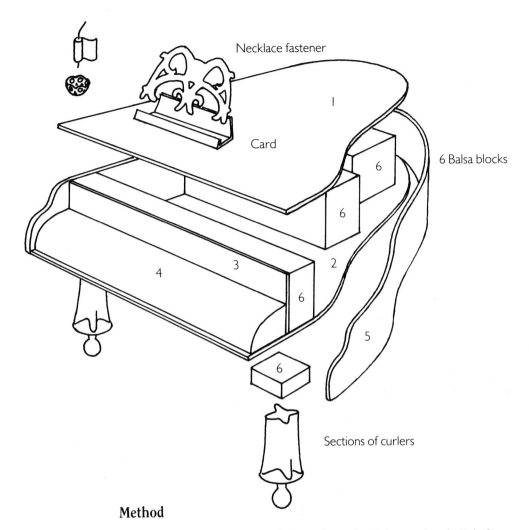

Necklace fastener

Card

6 Balsa blocks

Sections of curlers

## Method

1 Cut the two piano-shaped pieces from the shiny card and stick the longer top on to the shorter one.
2 Cut the piano base from balsa.
3 Use pieces of balsa to create space between the card tops and the balsa base (making a sandwich effect).
4 Cut the side of the piano from shiny card and stick it round the edges of the piano-shaped 'sandwich'.
5 Embed the Toni curler legs into blocks of balsa and stick to the under side of the base.
6 The front panel and lid are also cut from balsa and glued in place.
7 Spray the body of the piano brown.
8 Make the music rest from the necklace fastener and position on top of the piano.
9 Decorate the front panel with pieces of necklace fastener or bracelet link.
10 The candles are made from fine paper rolled round sewing cotton and placed in metal bead caps.
11 Finish off with the model railway fencing as the pedal rack.

# Indian Screen

I found a bracelet which boasted nine filigree links, each with an Indian motif, and was so charmed with them that I felt they should stay together. Mounted on card, they made a screen so expensive-looking that it has given rise to rumours concerning the Mem and the then Viceroy, to whom it once belonged.

## Method

1 Cut one central and two side panels.
2 Arrange links on the panels and draw round them.
3 Cut holes slightly smaller than the links.
4 Glue links in place to cover the holes.
5 Sew panels where indicated (as hinges).
6 Decorate top with doyley or jewellery.
7 Spray gold or silver.

Doyley

Card

Links

## Materials

*Links from a metal bracelet*
*Card*
*Necklace clasp*
*Broken jewellery or plastic*
*  doyley*
*Sewing cotton*

# Dining Room

*Although not as ornate as the Sitting Room, the Dining Room is still very much of its period. The 'mahogany' furniture is imposing and the chairs suitably elaborate. You could aim for a more 'cosy' effect, or something quite austere.*

# Tallboy

This type of furniture starts with a box. Use a ready-made box, or score some card and bend it to make the basic shape. Top this with layers of card or light wood and then embellish with columns and panelling. Unite the disparate items by spraying with an all-over colour.

## Method

1. Make or find a basic box.
2. Glue beads into place for feet.
3. Reinforce by adding extra back panel.
4. Glue links on front to form decorated panels.
5. Add strips of balsa wood to frame panels.
6. Use hair-curlers as columns. (Beads can extend curlers to fill space.)

## Materials

*Card or balsa wood*
*Home-perm curlers*
*Links from filigree bracelet*
*Beads*

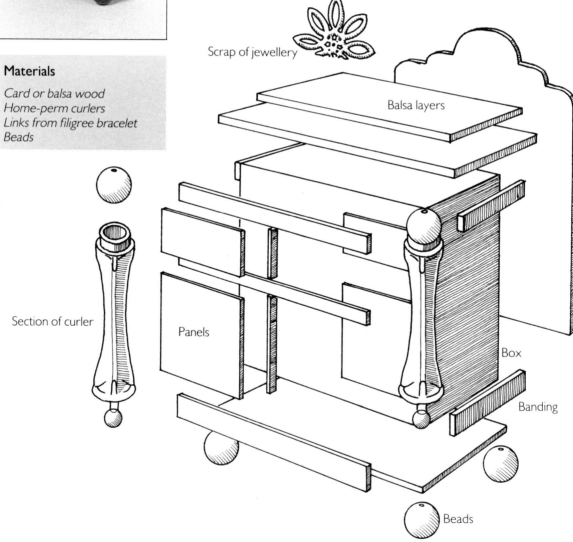

Scrap of jewellery

Balsa layers

Section of curler

Panels

Box

Banding

Beads

# Dining Table

**Materials**

*Souvenir gondola stand, or
   similar object
Piece of wood from cigar box
Car spray paint*

Have you seen those souvenir gondolas people bring back from Venice? I found a battered one still on its stand, and after I had discarded the boat the stand was wonderful as the base for a table.

**Method**

1 Place the wood on the stand to form the table top.
2 Spray the table with car enamel paint.

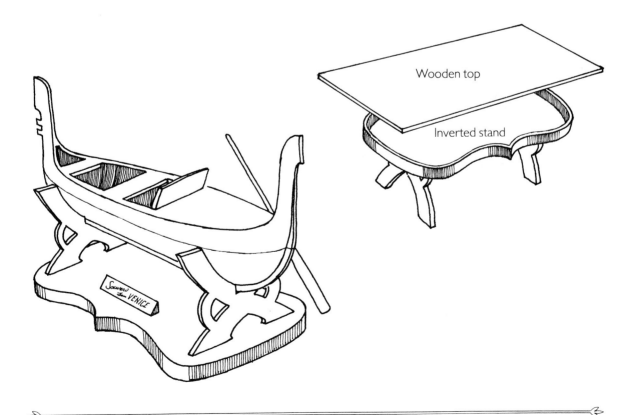

Wooden top

Inverted stand

# Chairs

Faced with the problem of making a matching set of chairs, I came up with the following solution: find a bracelet or chain belt with matching links!

## Method

1 From the light card, cut the two side frames, adapting the size to fit the links you are using.
2 Make two identical square seats, the first from light card, the second from balsa or heavier card.
3 Cover the second, heavier seat in the fabric, gluing all the rough edges in underneath.
4 Glue the link for the back in between the two side frames, reinforcing with matchstick (or card) struts above and below.
5 Put the seat made from light card in position (do *not* add the upholstered seat at this stage).
6 Add pieces of home-perm curler to make the legs more ornate.
7 Use paper-fastener heads for knobs (and detail on the back if you like).
8 Spray the chair brown with cellulose car paint.
9 When the frame is dry, glue the upholstered seat in place and finish off with cake trim foil, which will have to be painted by hand.

## Materials

*Light but firm cardboard*
*Filigree bracelet links*
*Home-perm curlers*
*Fine fabrics*
*Balsa or thick card*
*Paper-fastener heads*
*Foil cake-trim*
*Matchsticks*

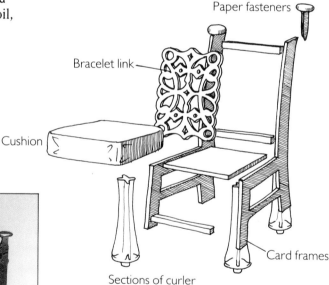

Paper fasteners

Bracelet link

Cushion

Card frames

Sections of curler

# Fireguard and Fire Irons

Everyone goes mad about these, I suppose because they are so charming. Although they are fiddly, they are easy to make and enhance a fireplace no end.

## Materials

*Nurse's type belt buckle*
*Half chain links*
*Buttons*
*Metal bead caps, perforated, in various sizes*
*Paper clip*
*Small paint brush*
*Tiny gold beads*
*Brass wire*
*Bits of filigree*

## Method

### Fireguard
This is simply half the nurse's belt buckle with a half chain link on the top as a handle and two more links as feet, or it could be mounted on a button.

### Shovel
Use a piece of metal from the foil, scoring and bending as shown. The handle is made from brass wire, a bead cap and little gold bead.

### Brush
The wire is the handle, with the paint-brush bristles enclosed in a bead cap for the head. Finish off the handle with a bead cap and tiny gold bead.

### Stand
A button is the base, with a deep bead on top and brass wire in the centre. Flatten a larger bead cap for the next stage and top it with a smaller cap and a tiny bead or two. Each of the irons engages in a slot.

### Tongs
These are basically part of a paper clip with a brass wire handle threaded through a bead and topped with a bead cap and further bead. Tiny bits of filigree go on the ends of the paper clip.

### Poker
A piece of brass wire with a bead cap and bead handle and another bead further down.

# Telephone

The servants' telephone was one of the few electrical 'contrivances' Major Rhodeahead tolerated in his home. Convinced the thing would leak electricity, he rarely used it himself and, if forced to, he would hold the earpiece well away from his head and then complain that you couldn't hear through it anyway! Servants being expendable, however, he was philosophical about installing a telephone in the servants' hall, and later one in the main hallway which was a more elegant affair altogether. How you make yours must be up to you, and I will content myself with an exploded drawing of one of mine which will show how the different pieces were put together. The example in the photograph is different again.

**Materials**

*Fluted bugle head*
*Tiny gold beads*
*Sequins*
*Opaque glass beads*
*Two halves of a chain link*
*Necklace clasp*
*Drawing pin*
*Cuff-link top*
*Four tiny beads*
*Brooch*
*Piece of thread*

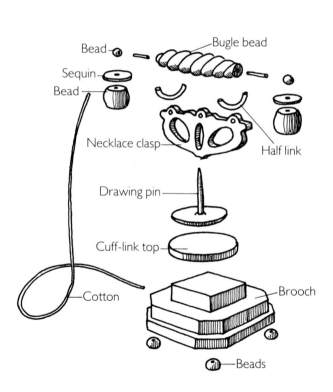

Bead

Bugle bead

Sequin

Bead

Necklace clasp

Half link

Drawing pin

Cuff-link top

Cotton

Brooch

Beads

## Method

1  The brooch is the base with a tiny bead at each corner.
2  On top of this goes the cuff-link top, the drawing pin and the necklace clasp.
3  The receiver is the fluted bugle bead with, at either end, an opaque glass bead with a sequin on top and a tiny bead on top of that.
4  The two halves of the chain link are positioned as shown and the cotton becomes the telephone wire.

# 8

# Hall

*In addition to practical objects such as the Hallstand and Umbrella Stand, the Hall is characteristically over-filled. The Suit of Armour and the Jardinière and Stand are typical of an age when every inch of space was used to display as many possessions as possible.*

# Hallstand

## Method

1 Following the exploded diagram, start with the buckle, cut as shown, for the base, and beads for feet.
2 Two fancy bracelet links form the central support and the matchbox makes the drawer part. Put a balsa wood strip on either side of the matchbox, and on top a table area also made of balsa wood.
3 Use a bent chain belt link on either side of the balsa wood strips.
4 The child's plastic hair slide forms the back with another bracelet link on top as the backing for the mirror.
5 Mount the small dental inspection mirror on the link.
6 Above the mirror goes the handbag clasp with paper-fastener heads on either side.
7 Finish off the drawer fronts with bead caps for handles.
8 A lolly stick formed the spine for the back of the stand and the whole thing apart from the mirror was sprayed white with cellulose car paint.

## Materials

*Matchbox*
*Balsa wood strips*
*Handbag clasp*
*Bracelet links*
*Dentist's inspection mirror*
*Paper fasteners*
*Plastic hair slide*
*Buckle*
*Beads and bead caps*
*Lolly stick*
*Links from chain belt*

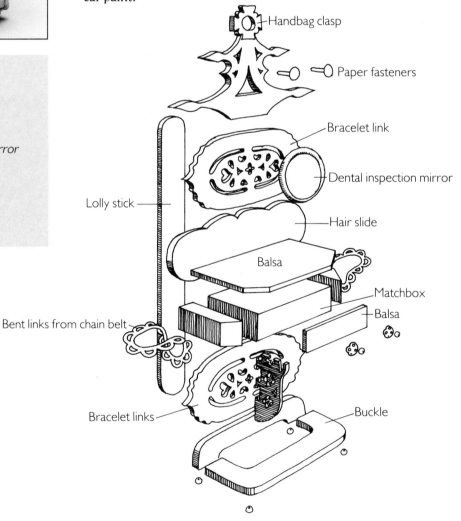

Handbag clasp

Paper fasteners

Bracelet link

Dental inspection mirror

Lolly stick

Hair slide

Balsa

Matchbox

Balsa

Bent links from chain belt

Bracelet links

Buckle

# Hats

After a lot of experiment I found this way to make hats.

**Method**

1 Remove the pills carefully from the bubble pack using a pin to avoid damaging the plastic 'domes'.
2 Cut out the crown-shaped bubbles to make the crowns of the hats.
3 Back them with circles cut from the card to make brims.
4 Trim with feathers, lace and sequins.

**Materials**

*Bubble packs for largish pills*
*Stiff card*
*Feathers, lace and sequins*

Card brim

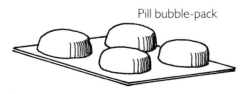

Pill bubble-pack

# Suit of Armour

I purloined the cat's bell to make a rather good helmet, and the fancy sword was a cocktail stick. Arm yourself with a good drawing before you tackle the armour.

## Method

1  Make pipe-cleaner figure, but substitute bell for head.
2  Add visor and mount figure on button.
3  Cut out individual pieces of armour and score any detail from the back so that it stands out.
4  Dress carefully, starting with arm pieces.
5  Follow with leg and neck pieces.
6  Add breastplate and skirt.
7  Add elbow, knee joins and gloves.
8  Stand the result in a dark corner. (The back will be less than perfect!)

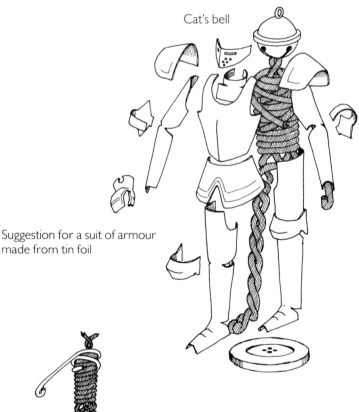

Cat's bell

Suggestion for a suit of armour made from tin foil

## Materials

*Pipe-cleaner figure (use bell instead of head)*
*Tin foil from takeaway container*
*Miniature sword*

Basic body built up from pipe-cleaners

# Umbrella Stand and Sticks

## Method

### Umbrella stand
Stick the lipstick tube on to the gilt button, which forms the base.

### Walking Sticks
Use a knitting needle of the right colour and thickness; make the handle by bending it to shape in boiling water, then cut to size. Finish off with a bead.

## Materials

*Lipstick case; gilt button*
*Fine-gauge knitting needle;*
  *gold bead; gold bead cap*

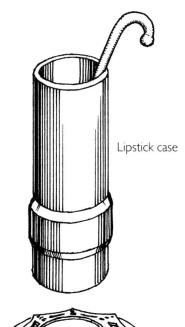

Lipstick case

Fancy button

Bead

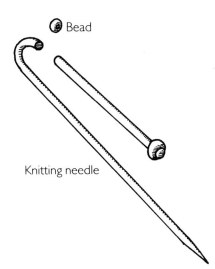

Knitting needle

# Hall Light

## Method

1 Make the central fixture using the brooch as the ceiling rose. Fix one of the medium bead caps to it, then a piece of drinking-straw, a smaller bead cap, two more medium caps face to face, and then the two large caps.
2 Stick these together in this order (the same sequence as shown in the exploded drawing), and finish off with some tiny beads.
3 The four identical lights are attached by horizontal wire 'arms', one at each quarter.
4 The sequence for each is: piece of straw, small bead cap, medium pearl, two more small bead caps, back to back, and lastly the smaller pearl.

### Materials

*Transparent drinking-straws*
*Two large bead caps*
*Four medium bead caps*
*Four medium-sized pearl beads*
*Four smaller pearl beads*
*Twelve small bead caps*
*Assorted smaller beads*
*Covered wire*
*Brooch*

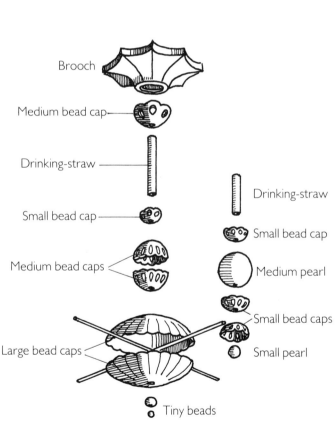

Brooch

Medium bead cap

Drinking-straw

Small bead cap

Medium bead caps

Large bead caps

Tiny beads

Drinking-straw

Small bead cap

Medium pearl

Small bead caps

Small pearl

# Jardinière and Stand

Even if you go late to a jumble sale, you may still be able to find the odd dressing-table drawer-handle and single chess pieces – in which case you are all set to make a jardinière, which is a variation on the bust on stand. If you have a glass handle, paint it white, decorate with motifs cut from gift-wrap paper, and there you are.

Now you need an aspidistra.

## Method

To make leaves of plant, cut a Harrods or other dark green plastic bag into either separate leaves or one long strip with irregular edges. In either case, glue one end to a pin, roll bag round the pin and stuff into the screw-hole of handle, then fluff out leaves and arrange.

Feeling that a castle went with a Harrods bag, that's what I used as the column for my stand.

## Materials

*Jardinière*
*Drawer-handle*
*Motifs from gift-wrap paper*
*Harrods bag*

**Stand**
*Buttons*
*Brooch*
*Chess castle*

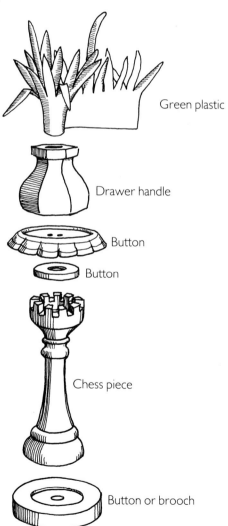

Green plastic

Drawer handle

Button

Button

Chess piece

Button or brooch

# 9

# Nursery

*A nursery in a dolls' house is a must because it is so much fun to make the toys and furniture to go in it. At Chipsand Place, the nursery is divided into two halves – the day nursery, which includes a play area and toys, and the night nursery, where visiting grandchildren sleep in a bed and a cot. Both are presided over by the nanny, Polly Esther.*

# Child's Bed

## Materials

*Plastic oval frame (or buckle)*
*Card or balsa wood*
*Balsa wood strips*
*Handbag clasp (or buckle)*
*Toni-type curlers*

## Method

1 Cut off oval plastic frame (or buckle) about two thirds down for bedhead.
2 Cut card or balsa wood to size for base.
3 Reinforce base with balsa wood strips and turn it over so they are underneath the bed.
4 Cut off the Toni curlers to form the bed legs and glue into place.
5 Make an upholstered pad to fill in the oval frame and glue for the bed head.
6 Attach handbag clasp (or a buckle) for the footboard.
7 Spray the whole bed brown.
8 Finish off with pillow and covers.

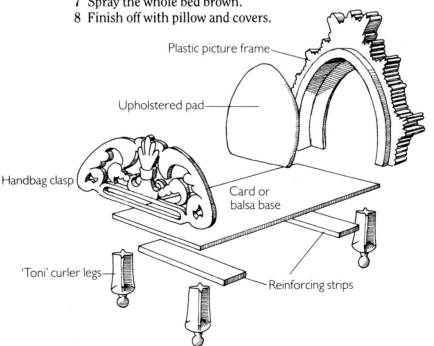

Plastic picture frame

Upholstered pad

Handbag clasp

Card or balsa base

'Toni' curler legs

Reinforcing strips

# Baby's Cot

The way I made this cot may seem rather eccentric, but I repeat – it all depends on what materials you have to hand. I had some curlers in my drawer, and at a local chemist there were some shampoo bottles in a plastic pre-stamped tray. They were happy to give me the tray, and this is how I made my cot.

## Method

1  Stick balsa strip across base of oval.
2  To make the legs, cut the ends off two of the plastic curler frames as shown and stick them at an angle, resting against the balsa strip.
3  Add press-studs as wheels.
4  Cross brace the legs.
5  Cut the third curler and glue on for the hood strut.
6  Gather a strip of lace-edged material and stick on to oval body.
7  Gather another strip of material to make the hood.
8  Fill cradle with lace-edged blanket.
9  Trim with rosebuds, or similar decoration.

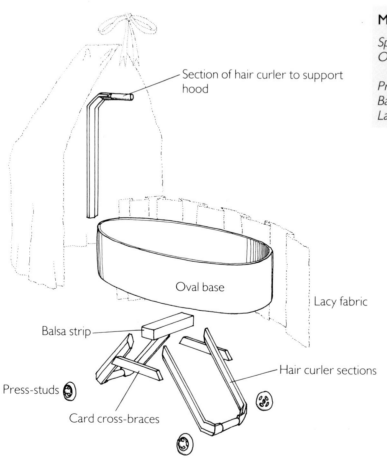

Section of hair curler to support hood

Oval base

Lacy fabric

Balsa strip

Press-studs

Card cross-braces

Hair curler sections

### Materials

*Sponge-type hair curlers*
*Oval shape (as from plastic tray described above)*
*Press-studs*
*Balsa wood strip*
*Lacy material*

# The Dolls' House Dolls' House

## Method

1 Copy the drawing of the flat house and score along the dotted lines.
2 Fold into a box shape and glue.
3 Fold all the tabs inwards.
4 Make the roof, score and fold.
5 Fold the forward edge over to make the barge board.
6 Attach the roof to the house by gluing it to the tabs.
7 Make the base from balsa wood or heavy card and glue the house to it.
8 Cut the chimney shape from balsa wood and use a tiny piece of straw for the pot.
9 The railway fence is bent round the base to finish off the model.

## Materials

*Heavy card or balsa wood*
*Stiff card*
*Model railway 00 gauge fencing*
*Plastic drinking-straw*

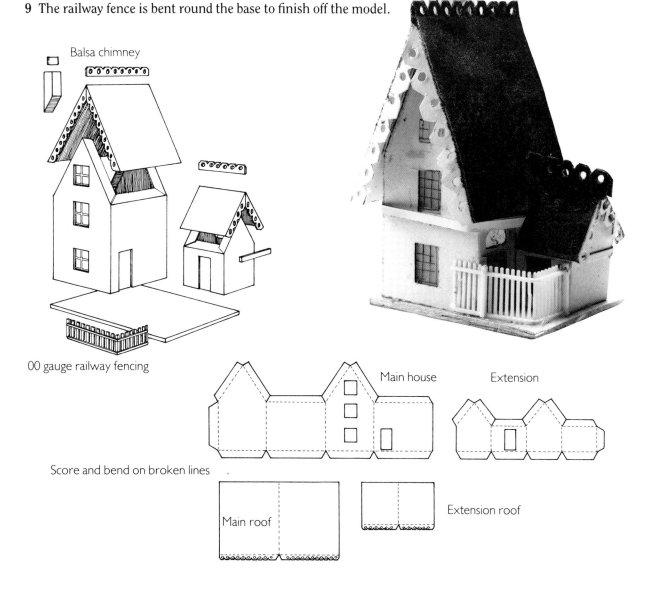

Balsa chimney

00 gauge railway fencing

Score and bend on broken lines

Main house

Extension

Main roof

Extension roof

# Jack-in-the-Box

Method

1 Make Jack from pipe cleaners, as shown, with a bead for a head.
2 Force the pipe-cleaner body into the Biro spring and make a little jacket from the fabric.
3 Make the box as shown in the illustration and stick the whole Jack into the box.

Bead

Pipe-cleaner body

Template for box

Biro spring

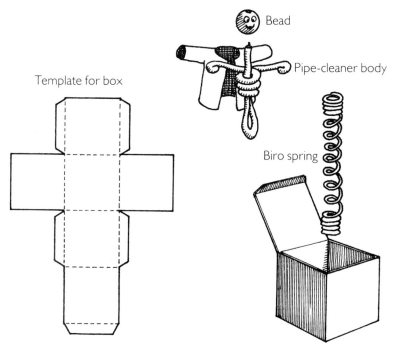

## Materials

*Bead*
*Pipe cleaners*
*Biro spring*
*Box*
*Fabric*

# Skipping Rope

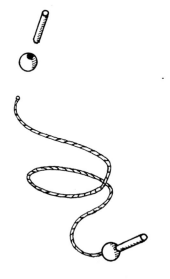

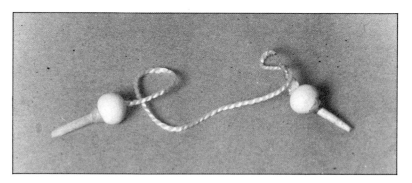

Method

1 The pieces of cocktail stick are the handles, with thread for the rope.
2 Finish off with beads for the knobs on the handles.

## Materials

*Pieces of cocktail stick*
*Beads*
*Thread*

# Push-along Horse

## Materials

*Balsa wood strip*
*Tiny buttons*
*Small beads*
*Matchsticks*
*Section of dowelling*
*Card*
*Feather*
*Half a link from a chain*
*Strips of coloured paper*
*String*

## Method

1  The balsa wood strip forms the base.
2  Use the four matchsticks for the legs with the tiny buttons for
   wheels, and the even tinier beads to cover the holes.
3  The section of dowelling forms the body, with the feather for a tail.
4  Cut the head from card, draw on the features and bridle, and insert
   it into a slit in the end of the dowelling.
5  Wrap strips of coloured paper round the body to finish.
6  Attach the half-link to the base and tie string to it to pull the horse
   along with.

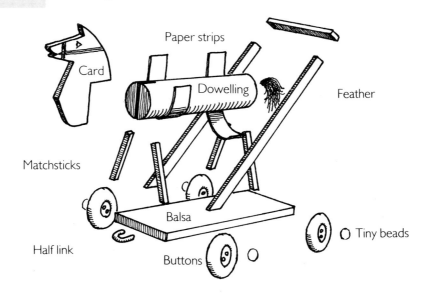

# Pedal Car

This car started with one of those boxes used to pack toothbrushes. I sat with a picture of a child's toy car in front of me as I made it.

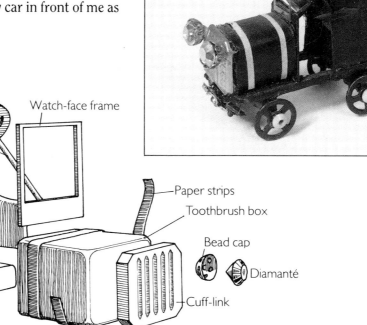

Cocktail stick — Watch-face frame

Seat

Bead — Paper strips — Toothbrush box — Bead cap — Diamanté — Cuff-link

Dress-stud

Stiff card

Toy wheels

## Method

1  Cut the base (chassis) from stiff card.
2  Use the toothbrush package for the bonnet, band it with strips of paper, and stick it to the base.
3  Use the dress-stud base for the grille, sticking it to the front of the bonnet.
4  Make the seat and its cushion in the same way as for Armchair, page 39, and stick in place.
5  The watch-face frame becomes the windscreen and is fixed to the bonnet.
6  Glue the axles with wheels to the chassis.
7  The steering wheel (spare toy car wheel) is attached to the cocktail stick and fixed to the back of the bonnet.
8  The headlights are bead caps with diamanté lamps set in them.
9  Make the horn from a piece of dress-stud with a bead attached.

## Materials

*Two axles with wheels from a toy car!*
*Stiff card*
*Toothbrush package*
*Dress-stud*
*Frame from square watch face*
*Bead*
*Bead caps*
*Diamanté*
*Spare wheel from toy car*

### *For the seat:*
*¼" balsa*
*Thin card*
*Cotton wadding*
*Fine fabric*
*Lampshade gimp*

# Toy Boats

## Materials

### Larger boat
*Balsa wood*
*Card*
*Drinking-straw*
*Pins*
*Thread*

### Smaller boat
*Balsa wood*
*Plastic 'stirrer' spoon*
*Drinking-straw*
*Beads*
*Link*

Method

### Larger boat
1  Cut the keel from balsa wood.
2  Stick an extra piece of balsa 'forward' with a section of straw inserted.
3  The canopy is scored folded paper with stripes drawn on.
4  Mount it on tiny strips of balsa or pieces of cocktail stick.
5  Dressmaking pins support the cotton rail.

### Smaller boat
1  Make the body of the boat from three layers of the plastic 'stirrer'.
2  Use balsa for the superstructure and a tiny wire bead link for rails.
3  The funnel is a straw.

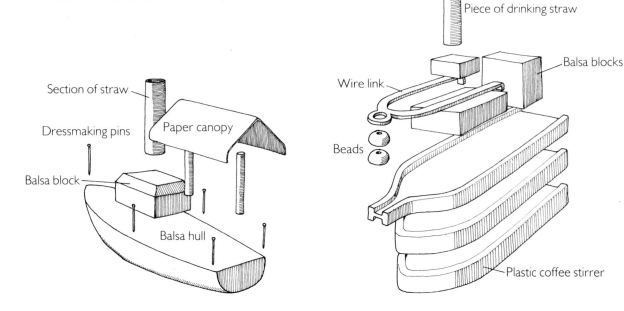

Section of straw

Dressmaking pins

Paper canopy

Balsa block

Balsa hull

Piece of drinking straw

Balsa blocks

Wire link

Beads

Plastic coffee stirrer

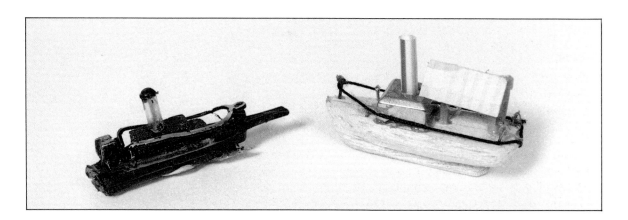

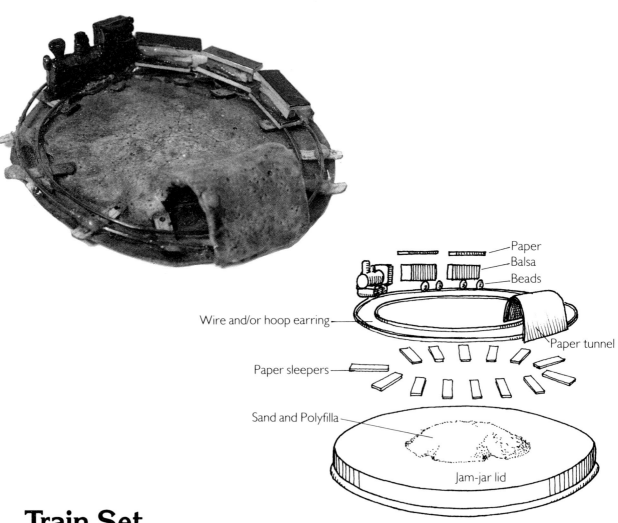

Paper
Balsa
Beads

Wire and/or hoop earring

Paper tunnel

Paper sleepers

Sand and Polyfilla

Jam-jar lid

# Train Set

This came about because a broken charm bracelet came my way and one of the charms was an engine. A thin jam-jar lid served as the layout to put the track on, the outer circle of which was a large hoop earring and the inner circle just wire. The sleepers were made from paper, as was the tunnel.

## Method

1  Make the track by laying the hoop earring or wire bent to the right shape on the jam-jar lid and the second circular piece of wire inside as inner track.
2  The sleepers and tunnel are made from paper and stuck in place.
3  Carriages are pieces of the balsa wood strip with paper roofs, and wheels made from either paper circles or beads.
4  Paint the scene with watercolours and sprinkle the ground with Polyfilla mixed with sand to give it texture.
5  Give the whole thing two coats of varnish.

### Materials

*Engine charm from bracelet or*
  *novelty from cracker*
*Jam-jar lid*
*Wire and/or hoop earring*
*Balsa wood strip*
*Polyfilla and sand*
*Circles of paper left by hole*
  *puncher or beads*
*Paper*
*Paint*
*Varnish*

# Three-wheeled Horse

To begin with, I actually traced this horse straight from its picture in a Victorian catalogue, for it was exactly the right size.

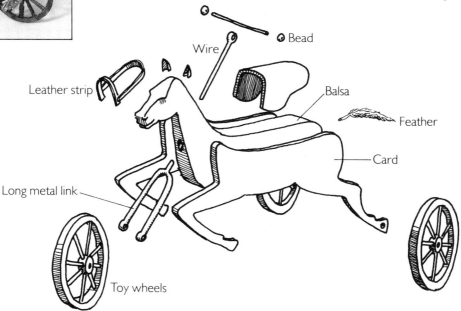

Bead

Wire

Leather strip

Balsa

Feather

Card

Long metal link

Toy wheels

## Materials

*Thin card*
*Balsa wood*
*Polyfilla*
*Wire*
*Long metal link*
*Small wheels*
*Tiny chain*
*Thin piece of dowel*
*Pieces of real or imitation leather (e.g. from an old diary)*
*Feather*
*Paint*

## Method

1 Copy the drawing and cut two horses out of thin card.
2 Sandwich a layer of balsa between them.
3 Make sure all four legs are separated and paint them with Polyfilla to stiffen them.
4 Spread the back legs, make a hole in the end of each and thread on to the thin dowelling axle.
5 Fix a wheel on either end of the axle.
6 Attach the front wheel to the body using either wire or a suitably shaped long metal link.
7 Insert wire up through the chest and head and attach a small piece of wire across the end of it, with a tiny bead on either end for a handle.
8 Paint the horse and add the feather for a tail.
9 Use the piece of leather and fine chain for harness.
10 The mane can either be painted on or made from cotton.

# Washstand

Washstands are indispensable pieces of Victorian furniture, and set the period very well. The one shown here started life as a broken plastic fan with a really awful picture on each elaborately scrolled section. The plastic made wonderfully ornate ironwork when sprayed white. The mirror was a doll's, and the lower shelf was a bracelet link. The jug was found as it is and so was the bowl. I sprayed both white.

## Method

1 Pieces cut from the plastic fan form the back and legs and are fixed to three sides of the bracelet link.
2 The paper-fastener box with a suitably sized hole cut in it sits on top of the legs and is backed with the plastic buckle.
3 Fix one half of the curtain ring to either side of the box and trim the front with plastic moulding.
4 Finish off the washstand by mounting the mirror on the back and putting the bowl and jug in place.

## Materials

*Plastic fan*
*Plastic buckle*
*Small paper-fastener box*
*Bowl*
*Small mirror*
*Curtain ring, cut in half*
*Bracelet link*
*Plastic moulding*
*White cellulose car spray paint*

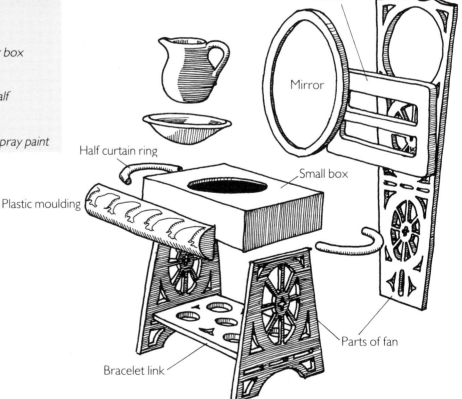

# Fire-screen

ere's where I give away my age: we used to have one, so I wanted to make a similar fire-screen for my dolls' house. I found that netting from a kitchen strainer worked well, and I used a child's bracelet for the brass rail. You can spiral wire by turning it in a brace and bit while holding the other end.

## Materials

*Metal bracelet*
*Sieve mesh*
*Spiralled wire*
*Card for base*

## Method

1 Cut rectangle in card for fire step.
2 Cut strip of mesh; bend for sides.
3 Glue round fire step.
4 Add upright wires.
5 Glue bracelet in place.
6 Glue guard rail in place.

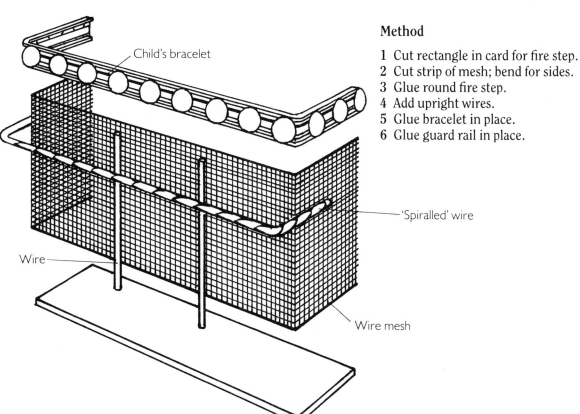

Child's bracelet

'Spiralled' wire

Wire

Wire mesh

# 10

# Bathroom

*Like many Victorian bathrooms, this is a converted bedroom. In the age of the relative youth of plumbing and sanitation, some very odd-looking devices were invented for dealing with the less mentionable aspects of civilized living. And inevitably, everything was given a highly decorative appearance.*

# Bath

The first bath I made was a pottery bowl thrown on the wheel and then cut down to hip-bath shape. However, I felt this wasn't fair to you so I set about exploring other ways to make a satisfactory bath. When I spotted the 1200 saccharin dispenser, I swooped on its bubble pack with shrieks of joy. It was clear plastic, and when I had cut the card backing off it and removed the contents, lo and behold, the most wonderful bath with lots of lovely moulding stood before me – I bore it off in triumph!

I do not quite know how Major Rhodeahead got into the bath, but I suddenly decided to make him and sit him there. Water was a problem solved by my son, who suggested I try fibreglass. I did, and when it dried there was the Major with water coming right up to his expectations! The colour is a bit odd though, and I have often been asked why it is so funny. I have always answered vaguely. "It's all the quinine they had to take in India to avoid malaria!"

## Materials

*Plastic bubble pack from*
*    saccharin dispenser*
*Balsa wood*
*Beads*
*Small metal washers*
*Moulding (from DIY shop,*
*    optional)*
*Press-studs*
*Glass button*
*Piece of eraser*
*Piece of chain*
*Bead cap*
*Gift-wrap motifs*
*White car spray paint*

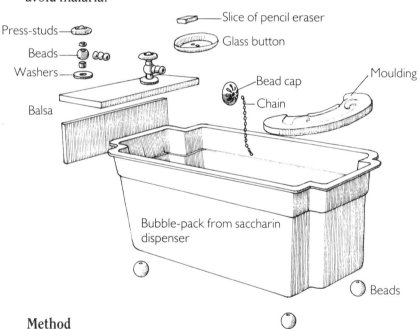

Press-studs

Beads

Washers

Balsa

Slice of pencil eraser

Glass button

Bead cap

Chain

Moulding

Bubble-pack from saccharin dispenser

Beads

## Method

1  Spray the bubble pack with white cellulose car paint and decorate with motifs.
2  Use beads for the bath feet.
3  The moulding trims the foot of the bath.
4  Use the balsa wood to make the shelf which supports the taps and the backing beneath.
5  The taps are made from the small metal washers, press-studs and beads.
6  Use a bead cap and the piece of chain for the plug fitting.
7  Finish off the piece with the glass button and a slice of eraser for soap in the soap-dish.

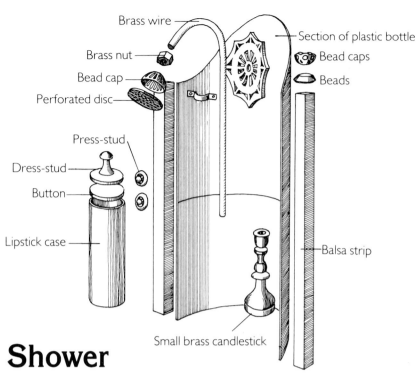

**Materials**

*Medium-weight cardboard or
    part of washing-up-liquid
    bottle
Thin balsa wood
Silver-coloured paper cake-trim
    or fancy gift-wrap paper
Perforated disc (from old-
    fashioned beaded earring)
Brass wire
Miniature brass candlestick (e.g.
    from Cluedo) or similar
    brass-coloured fitting
Brass nut
Brooch
Brass lipstick case
Dress-stud
Beads
Brass wire
Piece of chain link*

# Shower

Victorian showers were fascinating. Looking through all the pictures I could find of them, I chose to reproduce the one in which the bather apparently stood up in his bath and pumped vigorously on a cylinder beside the bath and, when the vacuum built up sufficiently, a volume of water fell on his head (mine not to reason whether it was hot or cold).

For the taps, look out for plastic stretch necklaces with 'beads' like this ꧁. Top them with bead caps or small press-studs.

## Method

1  Make the shower stall either from a washing-up-liquid bottle cut to shape, or from cardboard cut to shape and curved, with a thin strip of balsa supporting either side of the entrance.
2  Decorate the stall with either the cake-trim or gift-wrap.
3  The water pipe and base are made from the tiny brass candlestick topped with a combination of small brass-coloured beads, and the brass wire runs up the back of the stall. It is curved over at the top and fixed in place with the piece of chain link.
4  The shower head is made from the perforated disc (in this case taken from an old-fashioned earring) placed in the opening of a large bead cap which is attached to the end of the wire water pipe. The join is concealed with a brass nut.
5  Decorate the tops of the balsa supports with small beads and bead caps.
6  The brooch is positioned behind the top of the wire pipe.
7  The taps fixed to the balsa support are made from those semi-transparent flower-shaped beads found on stretch necklaces, but you could improvise with a combination of fancy beads, bead caps and press-studs.
8  The brass lipstick case stands by the side of the shower with a bead and the dress-stud to top it off.

# Water Closet

By far my favourite of all the things I have made is this water closet. Mine stands, as befits its status, on a raised throne reached by steps. It is very rewarding to make.

## Method

1 For the cistern, cut the butter container in half as shown. Place the top half on the bottom half and stick.
2 Cut the base and back of the cistern shelf from card, score, bend, and fix cistern in place.
3 Make up the seat from shapes cut from card as shown, and stick to the milk container loo.
4 Two bugle beads form the hinges and the backing is cut from card.
5 Fix the cistern to the loo with the straw and plastic nozzle.
6 Cut the necklace clasp in two to form the fancy brackets.
7 Bend a piece of wire to make the flush bar, and attach the chain with a handle made from beads.
8 For a final touch, turn over another butter container and you will find a lovely little shield emblazoned there. Cut it out and stick it to the cistern front.

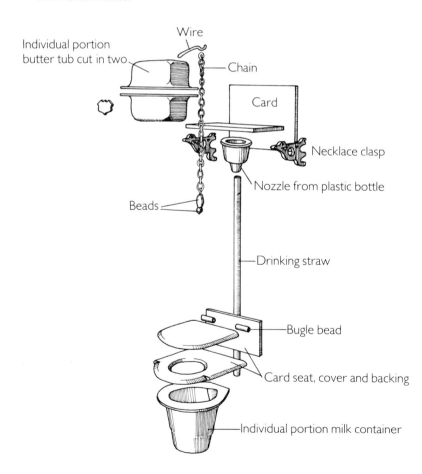

Individual portion butter tub cut in two

Wire

Chain

Card

Necklace clasp

Nozzle from plastic bottle

Beads

Drinking straw

Bugle bead

Card seat, cover and backing

Individual portion milk container

## Materials

*Stiff card*
*Individual plastic butter*
    *container*
*Plastic drinking-straw*
*Nozzle from plastic bottle*
*Individual milk container*
*Necklace clasp*
*Wire*
*Fine chain*
*Beads, including two bugle*
    *beads*

# Jug on Stand

Sometimes a piece of dolls'-house crockery appears in a jumble sale. This one was plastic, so I sprayed it white then decorated it with a motif from gift-wrap paper. The stand came about simply from sticking together a string of things I had in my treasure box. You may decide to do it differently, depending on what makings you have. I hope mine will start you off.

### Method

1 The exploded drawing shows the sequence of materials for building the stand.
2 Spray the whole thing white with car spray paint.

## Materials

*Brooch*
*Button*
*Cake candle-holder (top left over from making Servants' Bells, see page 89)*
*Plastic perforated bead*
*Earring minus central stone*
*Button*
*Part of filigree bracelet*
*White car spray paint*

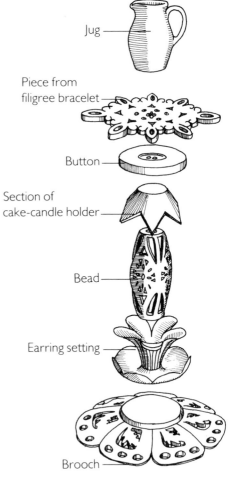

Jug

Piece from filigree bracelet

Button

Section of cake-candle holder

Bead

Earring setting

Brooch

# Oil Heater

These look wonderful in any room and give an authentic-looking atmosphere. They are also good presents and take only minutes to make.

## Materials

*Metal cigar tube*
*Brooch or button of the same diameter*
*Bead cap of the same diameter*
*Earring minus central stone*
*Embossed cake-trim foil*
*Wire*
*Bugle bead*
*Tiny bead caps*
*Tiny bead*

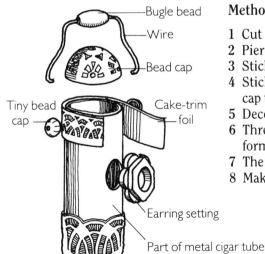

Bugle bead
Wire
Bead cap
Tiny bead cap
Cake-trim foil
Earring setting
Part of metal cigar tube
Button or brooch

## Method

1 Cut the rounded end off the tube and cut the cylinder down to size.
2 Pierce a hole in the front.
3 Stick on the earring to frame the hole (or use a piece of doyley).
4 Stick on either the brooch or button for the base, and the bead cap top.
5 Decorate the top and bottom of the heater with embossed foil.
6 Thread the wire through the bugle bead, bent as in the drawing, to form the handle.
7 The ends of the wire go through the holes in two small bead caps.
8 Make the central knob from a bead cap and tiny bead.

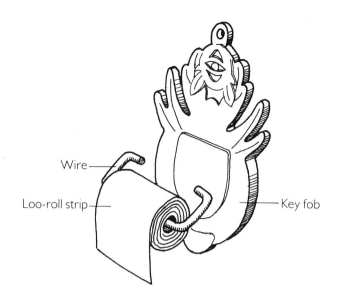

Wire

Loo-roll strip

Key fob

# Loo-roll Holder

The holder shown here was made from a pendant, but you could use a key fob.

## Method

1 Roll up the strip cut from the loo roll.
2 Insert a piece of wire through the centre.
3 Wire it on to the pendant or key fob.

**Materials**

*Pendant or key fob*
*Strip cut from loo roll*
*Wire*

# 11

# Kitchen

*The turn-of-the-century kitchen is always a fascinating place, again exhibiting the beginnings of 'technology', but retaining many old-fashioned practices.
The Dresser, Kitchen Range and Crockery give the room real character, but there is enormous potential for all kinds of obscure shiny devices and objects with uncertain functions and intriguing appearances.*

**Materials**

*Stiff card*
*Bead caps*
*Paper-fastener heads*

# Kitchen Dresser

The basic shape was made from card and the twiddly-bits are bead caps squashed flat. The handles are tops of paper-fasteners. See page 90 for how to make the crockery.

### Method

1 Cut all the basic shapes out of card, and score and bend the main part into shape as shown.
2 Slot in the two long upper shelves, the broad shelf in the middle, and the bottom shelf.
3 Build up the drawer facings from pieces of card and stick the drawer panel in place, and the upper moulding.
4 Spray the whole thing a uniform colour.
5 Finish off with the squashed bead caps and paper-fastener heads for drawer handles.

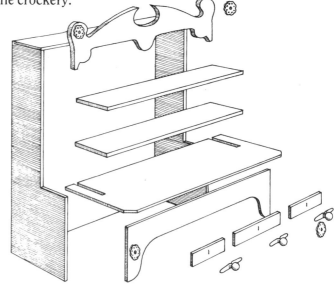

# Oven

There are many variations on this basic model, and you could come up with something quite different, depending on the pieces you have to hand.

### Method

1  Cut the box shape for the oven from the card following the diagram. The oven top is also cut from card.
2  Use balsa wood for the centre door panel.
3  The ventilator is a metal scarf ring opened out and set into the space above the door.
4  Make the door hinges from metal foil, pierced with a pin to indicate rivets, or use rows of small beads as shown in the Kitchen Range, page 187.
5  The door handle is a link and the front of the door can be decorated with a piece of bracelet link.
6  The oven top can be finished off with either a buckle, or the textured base from something like a plastic fish container, which has an interesting bobbly surface.
7  The gas taps and pipe are made from wire and bead caps and attached to the side of the oven.
8  Finish off the bottom of the door with a fancy link or bead cap.

### Materials

*Card*
*Balsa wood*
*Buckle*
*Chain links, of various sizes and types*
*Metal foil food container*
*Bead caps*
*Wire*
*Beads*
*Bracelet links*

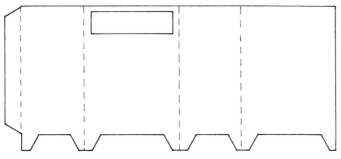

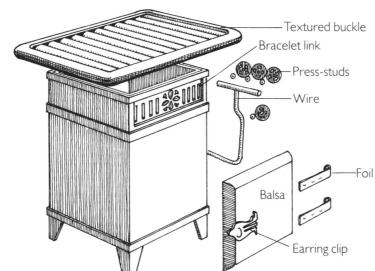

Textured buckle
Bracelet link
Press-studs
Wire
Foil
Balsa
Earring clip

# Kitchen Range

I was horrified to hear that these can be as much as £40 to buy! I have had more requests for instructions about making kitchen ranges than anything else, except perhaps the loo (see page 79). So here you are.

## Method

1 Following the diagram, cut out the body of the range from the medium-weight card, scoring the folding lines. Bend and make up as shown.
2 From the manila card, cut the top plates and small oven door panels.
3 Use the balsa for the feet. Cut two to the shape shown.
4 Cut the main oven door from the balsa.
5 The top and base are cut from balsa or heavy card. Stick them to the top and bottom of the body of the stove, then attach the feet to either end.
6 The three plates are stuck to the top of the range, the centre one covered with metal foil.
7 The chimney is constructed from the cartridge case with a piece of dowel or a pencil inside it.
8 Cut out the fire shelf and bars from medium card and stick them in position.
9 The main oven door, made from the balsa shape, has the brooch stuck to it, and the handle and hinges are made from a paper-fastener head and beads.

### Materials

Manila card, medium weight
Beads
Balsa wood
Metal foil from food container
Fancy foil cake-trim
Metal links and loops
Cartridge case
Pencil or dowel
Paper-fastener head
Brooch
Brass wire
Split pins

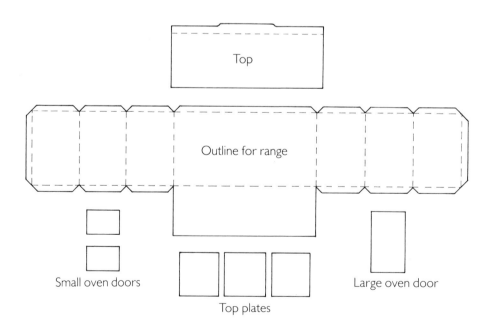

Top

Outline for range

Small oven doors

Top plates

Large oven door

10 The rail is brass wire, attached with split pins and bent as shown.
11 The cake-trim goes at the bottom of the centre space.
12 The two small oven doors are positioned as shown, with jewellery loops and links on the lower one, and the tap (made as for the Geyser, page 101) on the upper.
13 All the parts, except metal ones, should be spray-painted black as you go along.

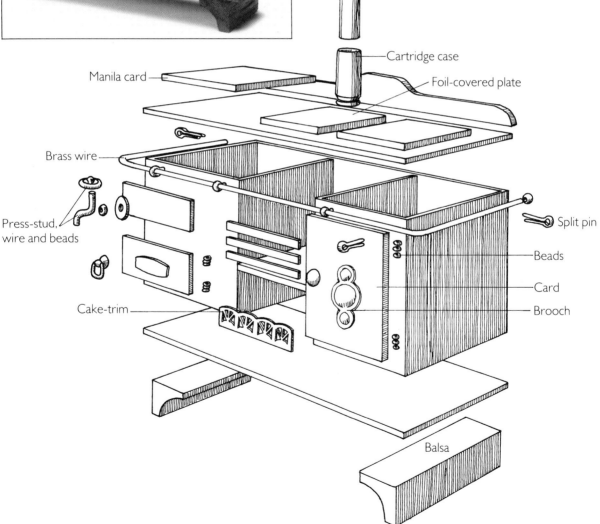

Dowel

Cartridge case

Manila card

Foil-covered plate

Brass wire

Press-stud, wire and beads

Split pin

Beads

Card

Brooch

Cake-trim

Balsa

# Servants' Telephone

## Method

1 Using the diagrams for guidance, cut the back, shelf, brackets and cover from the card.
2 Glue the brackets and shelf into place on the back piece.
3 Fix the balsa oblong beneath the shelf as shown and make the 'bells' from the heads of two of the paper fasteners.
4 Use either the tinfoil container or the brass shim to make the 'metal' plates above the shelf and fix them to the back.
5 Cut through the shaft of one of the paper fasteners and glue its head to the top 'plate'.
6 Attach the press-stud to the cut ends of the paper fastener for the mouthpiece.
7 Make the earpiece from half the necklace fastener and the string. Attach it to the telephone after threading the string through a bead cap to hide the joint.
8 Glue the card cover to the top of the phone.
9 Stick another paper fastener to the back of the phone, so that its head is visible from the front, and top it off with the tiny gold head as a finial.
10 Finish off with paper for notes on the shelf and the piece of dowelling as a pencil.

## Materials

*Card (for back, shelf, brackets and cover)*
*Brass shim (from model railway shop) or foil food container*
*Small strip of balsa wood*
*Paper fasteners*
*Press-studs*
*Screw-type necklace fastener*
*Tiny gold bead*
*Bead cap*
*Cotton*
*Paper*
*Tiny piece of dowel*

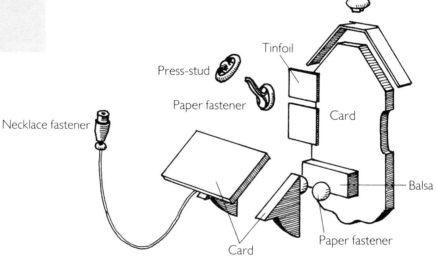

Necklace fastener

Press-stud

Paper fastener

Tinfoil

Card

Balsa

Paper fastener

Card

# Servants' Bells

**M**ajor Rhodeahead will not use the telephone as he is convinced the electricity escapes and affects his health. He insisted that servants' bells were fitted, but he had some time to wait while I solved the problem. I was prowling the wedding department of a large store in search of tiny bells when the solution offered itself. I noticed that the centre part of cake candle-holders are just the right shape, and can be bought in silver and gold.

### Method

1 Cut the candle-holders into three sections, using the middle piece for the 'bell'.
2 Insert a small bead into each bell.
3 Cut backing panel from card or balsa wood.
4 Stick medium beads on to card or wood backing.
5 Use strips of foil to suspend bells from beads.
6 Add detail to backing using strips of card or foil.

### Materials

*Cake candle-holders*
*Beads, small and medium*
*Foil (e.g. from metal food container)*
*Stiff card or balsa wood*

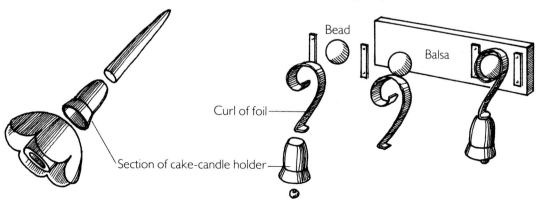

Bead

Balsa

Curl of foil

Section of cake-candle holder

# Crockery

I was appalled when I saw how expensive dolls'-house crockery was to buy, so I was forced to solve the problem of how to make it. After a lot of trial and error, I finally found pottery to be too clumsy. The answer was to use Barbola paste, which is a self-hardening modelling material.

## Materials

*Barbola paste*
*Buttons*
*Vaseline*
*Paint*
*Varnish*
*Cake candle-holders*
*Link from chain*

## Method

### Plates

1 Roll out Barbola paste thinly.
2 Cut or stamp out circles or ovals.
3 Press the 'plates' on to Vaselined buttons to give the correct shape.
4 When dry, remove the buttons.
5 Paint the plates and varnish them. (Wash brushes in turps or white spirit to prevent them hardening.)

### Porcelain cups

1 Make cups from part of cake candle-holders with half a link added for a handle.

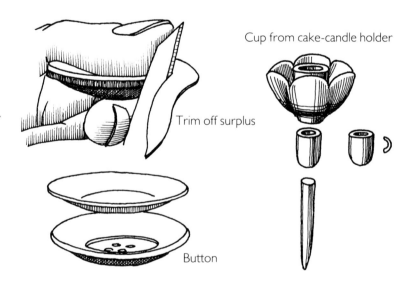

Cup from cake-candle holder

Trim off surplus

Button

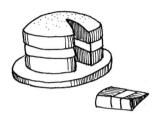

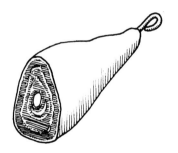

# Food

The food is made from salt dough, the recipe for which is below. You can model wonderfully realistic food from it by shaping, baking and painting. It lasts virtually for ever and you can incorporate wires and beads, or twist cotton round it at intervals for sausages. Use different finishes for a mouth-watering appearance.

### Method

1 Combine all the ingredients and knead to a flexible dough.
2 Model to desired shape, crimping the edges of 'pies', stamping out shapes, or simply rolling into balls then flattening them.
3 Bake as for pastry for about 15 minutes at 180°C/350°F/Gas Mark 4 until golden.
4 When cool, paint with watercolours or felt pen and varnish. (Wash the varnish brush in white spirit.)
5 Use Polyfilla as icing sugar, or for a sugared look sprinkle salt on the varnish while it's still wet.
6 Use the buttons as plates for the food.

### Materials

**Salt Dough**
*100 g plain flour*
*1 dessertspoon salt*
*Water to mix*

**Decoration**
*Beads*
*Buttons*
*Wire*
*Paint*
*Varnish*
*Polyfilla*
*Salt*

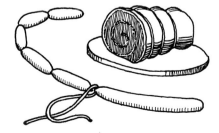

# Saucepans

The most convincing metal saucepans can be made, and while the plastic ones are very good, a set of brass ones gleam in a lovely way. I have taken to buying Marks and Spencer's lasagne as much for its brass-coloured foil as for the taste. Army buttons make wonderfully convincing lids, as they have writing round them as did much Victorian proprietary kitchenware.

## Materials

*Button with shaft*
*Plain button*
*Torch battery (of same diameter as buttons)*
*Hooks and eyes*
*Foil from food container*
*Ring from chain*

## Method

1 Cut a strip of foil long enough to go round the battery.
2 Wrap the foil around the battery and stick it to itself (i.e. not to the battery).
3 Insert the plain button and secure it to make the base.
4 Remove the 'saucepan' from the battery.
5 Insert the other button, shaft uppermost, to make the lid, and glue it in place.
6 Bend the 'eyes' as shown and glue them in place.
7 Cut the handles from the crimped edge of the foil.
8 Stick the handle to the other side of the pan and the ring round the base of the handle.

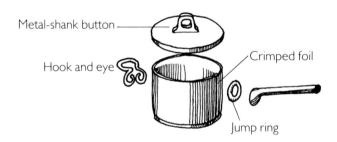

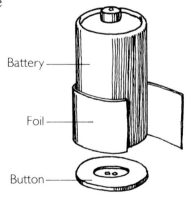

# Canisters

### Materials

*Toothpaste tops or insulator caps (from ironmongers)*
*Buttons with shafts*
*Paper for 'lining' and labels*

A set of these would make a nice present for someone with a dolls' house.

**Method**

1 Stick the buttons shaft-side up on the caps or tops (the buttons must fit them!).
2 For decorative 'lining', draw lines on a length of writing paper, cut to length and wrap round top of canister. (This is much easier than trying to draw on a cylinder!)
3 Draw labels on paper, then cut out and stick to canisters.

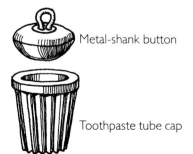

Metal-shank button

Toothpaste tube cap

Button

Insulation cap

Paper label

# Cruet

Here they are, straight from the catalogue of the day. Simply find the right makings and stick them together as illustrated.

### Method

1 Remove the pin and hook from the brooch and turn it upside down for the cruet base.
2 Position the faceted beads and bead caps as shown.
3 Add the 'eye' as a handle.

### Materials

*Diamanté brooch*
*Large 'eye' (from coat-size hook and eye)*
*Diamond-faceted beads*
*Tiny metal bead caps*

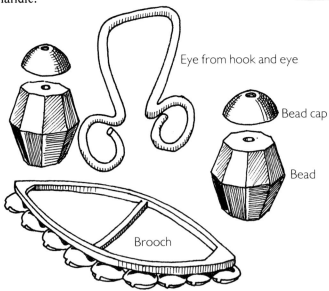

Eye from hook and eye

Bead cap

Bead

Brooch

# Knives and Breadboard

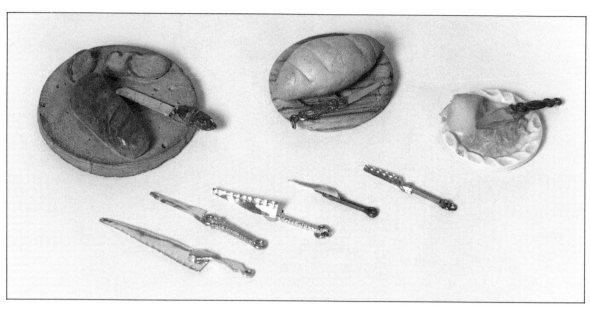

## Method

### Bread Knife

1 To make the blade, fold a sliver of foil over a comb and run a pencil over one edge to give a serrated edge. This is best done before the knife is cut to shape.
2 Slip the blade into a long bead to form a handle, or enclose it in Fimo.
3 The fine lines round the handle are made by binding with cotton.

### Materials

*Foil from food container*
*Link from chain*
*Long bead or Fimo*

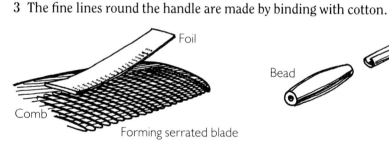

Foil

Bead

Link

Comb

Forming serrated blade

### Cheese Knife

1 Cut the blade as for the bread knife.
2 Make the 'antique' handle from a 'blocked in' link of a chain (though these are quite rare).

### Bread Board

Made from a slice cut from a large cork.

### Cheese

1 The hunk of cheese is a chunk cut from a yellow eraser.
2 The grated cheese is tiny snippets of yellow cotton.

Instructions for the bread are on page 91.

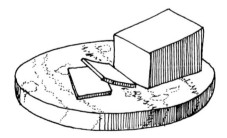

Cheese knife with 'cheese' from pencil eraser and cheeseboard from slice of cork

# Food Grinder

Actually, I'm not sure quite what this is, but there is one illustrated in an early 'Mrs Beeton's' and that's good enough for me. I suspect that it was the Victorian equivalent of a food processor. Anyway, I made it and it looks impressive hanging on the pantry wall.

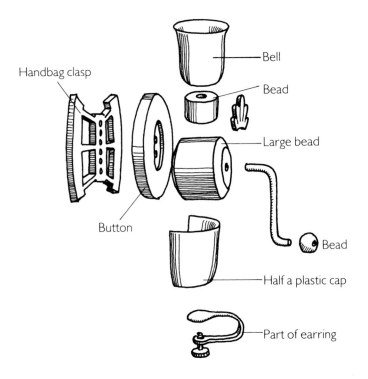

Handbag clasp

Bell

Bead

Large bead

Button

Bead

Half a plastic cap

Part of earring

## Materials

*Plastic bell*
*Handbag clasp*
*Button*
*Beads of various sizes*
*Half a plastic cap (from a bottle or tube)*
*Earring bits*
*Watch winder*
*Wire*

## Method

The sequence of parts in the construction of the grinder is shown in the exploded drawing. Assemble all the elements and attach the winder, made from wire and a bead, to the front.

## Materials

### Light with bells
Bead caps of different sizes
Beads, large and small
Fish hook
Bell-shaped beads
Glass 'diamond' beads
Pierced metal 'bucket' shape
 (e.g. from drop earring)

### Light with beads
Fancy brass button
Bead caps of different sizes
Beads, large and small
Cylinder bead
Fish hook
Pieces of transparent drinking-
 straw

# Ceiling Lights

Both the light with beads and the light with bells have fish
hooks for arms. I mentioned on page 46 that I had found some
bell-shaped beads which would also make splendid gas lamps, but
round beads can also look good.

### Method

The method of assembling the materials for both types of light is
shown in the exploded diagram.

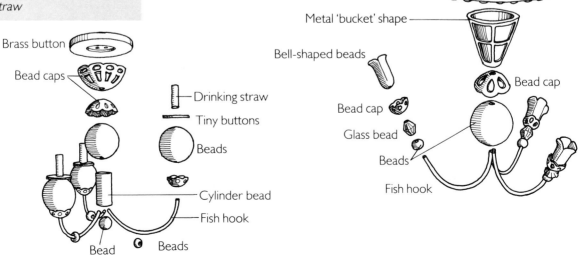

# 12

# Scullery

*The Scullery is something of a contrast to the cheerful warmth of the Kitchen and the overall comfort and opulence of the rest of the house. There is plenty of evidence of prosperity, but pity the poor maids who had to heave the coal hod, work the mangle and scrub the floors – this is very much a place of hard labour! Many objects from the Ironmonger could swap with the Scullery.*

# Stone Sink

## Method

### Materials

*Container for a single portion of butter (as found in any café)*
*Plastic press-studs or double beads*
*Wire*
*Balsa wood*

1 From the balsa wood, cut supports for either end of the butter tub, and one more support to hold up the draining board. Stick the tub between the supports.
2 Face the front of the tub with a scored piece of balsa.
3 Make the draining board from balsa wood, also scored to make water runs.
4 The taps are made from wire, with plastic press-studs or double beads for tap tops.
5 Stick a press-stud in the sink for a soakaway hole.
6 The 'soap' is a piece of yellow eraser on a button 'soap dish'.

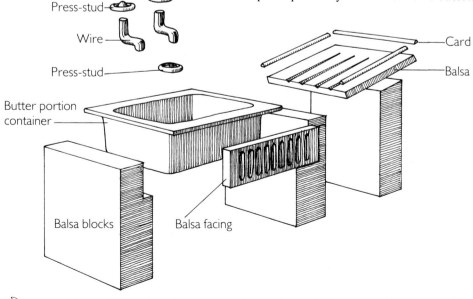

Press-stud
Wire
Press-stud
Butter portion container
Balsa blocks
Balsa facing
Card
Balsa

# Geyser and Coal Hod

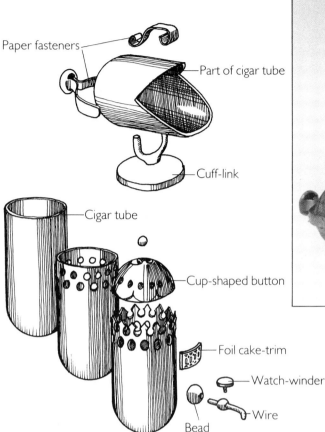

Paper fasteners

Part of cigar tube

Cuff-link

Cigar tube

Cup-shaped button

Foil cake-trim

Watch-winder

Bead

Wire

## Method

### Geyser

1 Cut the cigar tube to size for the geyser body.
2 Make two rows of staggered perforations.
3 Cut the edge into points.
4 Insert the cup-shaped button into the top of the tube and add the bead.
5 Stick the cake-trim on to the tube for detail.
6 Spray the whole thing silver or gold.
7 Add the tap, which is made from wire and the watch winder or bead cap.

### Coal hod

1 Cut the other half of the cigar tube to shape (easy with scissors).
2 Cut off the top of a cuff-link.
3 Stick the 'hod' on to the cuff-link 'stand' at a slight tilt.
4 Open up one paper fastener (to look like John Wayne's legs!) and attach to the back of the hod.
5 Remove the head from the other paper fastener and bend the prongs for the top handle.

## Materials

### Geyser
Cigar tube, preferably metal, but plastic will do
'Cup-shaped' button of same diameter as tube .
Wire
Bead
Watch winder or bead cap
Foil cake-trim
Silver or gold spray paint

### Coal hod
Cigar tube
Cuff-link
Paper fasteners

# Mangle

Finding the big wheel for this was the hard part, but it turned up unexpectedly as the base of something else which was quickly cannibalized. The inspiration for making the mangle came originally from the filigree metal links of a bracelet which I was sure would make marvellous side struts.

## Materials

*Metal bracelet links*
*Cardboard*
*Paper*
*Broad hoop earring,*
    *opened out*
*Glue-tube screw*
*Watch wheels with milled edges*
*Press-studs*
*Wire*
*Bead caps*
*Screw-type necklace fastener*
*Piece of cocktail stirrer*
*Beads*
*Wheel*

## Method

1  Cut the sides and shelf from cardboard.
2  Use the bracelet links as struts at either side and for the bottom shelf part.
3  The paper rolled into cylinders forms the rollers which sit between the struts on the top shelf.
4  Over the top of the rollers go the two sections of hooped earrings with the glue-tube screw in the centre.
5  Fix the necklace clasp to one of the watch wheels and fix that to one side of the mangle.
6  The other watch wheel goes at the other side with a bead between it and the big wheel. Another bead goes on the outside of the big wheel and a piece of cocktail stirrer makes the little handle.
7  A bead cap with a piece of curved wire on either side goes under the top shelf.
8  Finish off with press-studs for wheels.

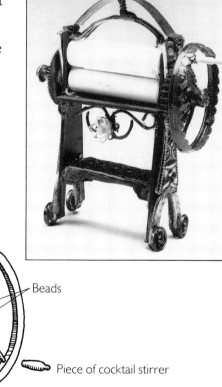

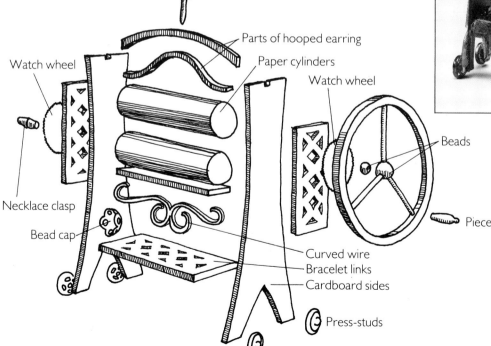

Glue-tube screw

Parts of hooped earring

Paper cylinders

Watch wheel

Watch wheel

Beads

Necklace clasp

Piece of cocktail stirrer

Bead cap

Curved wire

Bracelet links

Cardboard sides

Press-studs

# Dust Extractor

All the vacuum cleaners in the days before electricity were
wonderfully fussy-looking inventions, full of lovely knobs and
twiddly-bits, but I fell for this particular dust extractor because of
its brass dome. It was operated by two maids, one of whom stood
on the 'sled' part and, seizing the pole in both hands, pumped like
mad, while the other one manipulated the nozzle.

## Materials

### Sled
*Stiff card or balsa wood*

### Extractor dome
*Part of spring from Biro refill
Bead cap
Brass cylinder
Domed brass button (of same
    diameter as the cylinder)
Two 'eyes' (from hooks and
    eyes)
Flat brass button*

### Other parts
*Balsa wood
Card
Gold-coloured foil
Perforated brass bead cap
Glue-tube screw or screw eye
Mapping pen handle or part of
    knitting needle
Part of cuff-link
Part of dress-stud
Thin brass tube
Cord
Various bits of necklace
    fastener, bead caps
    and beads
.22 brass cartridge*

## Method

### Sled
1  Cut the shapes shown in the illustration from balsa or stiff card.
   There will be two sides, two cross pieces, and the stand where the
   'pumping' maid would be.
2  Glue all the pieces together to form the sled.

### Extractor Dome
1  Using the brass cylinder, the domed button and the flat brass
   buttons, follow the instructions for Saucepans, page 92, to make
   the cylinder. The flat button is the base.
2  The 'eyes' are the handles and the bead cap with the bit of Biro
   spring inside goes on top.

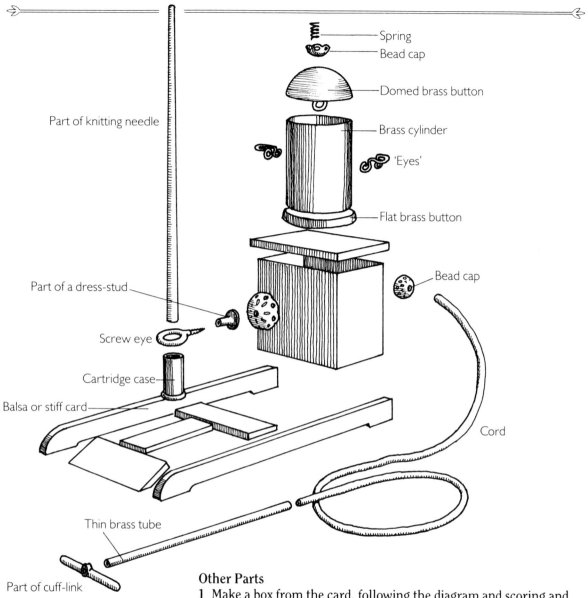

Part of knitting needle

Spring

Bead cap

Domed brass button

Brass cylinder

'Eyes'

Flat brass button

Bead cap

Part of a dress-stud

Screw eye

Cartridge case

Balsa or stiff card

Cord

Thin brass tube

Part of cuff-link

### Other Parts

1 Make a box from the card, following the diagram and scoring and bending as shown.
2 Use the balsa wood to make a top for the box and cover it with the gold foil.
3 The perforated brass bead cap is fixed to the front of the box and the screw eye, threaded through part of a dress-stud, is fixed to it.
4 The cartridge case is the seating for the pole and is slotted through the ring of the screw eye and fixed to the cross piece. The pole, either the knitting needle or pen handle, goes in the case.
5 Decorate the 'stand' part with a bit of link or filigree at either end.
6 The cord is attached to the side of the box with a bead or bead cap covering the join.
7 At the other end of the cord are the thin brass tube and the bar part of the cuff-link.
8 Trim the machine with odd bits of filigree, beads and paper-fastener heads for rivets and so forth.

# Washing Machine

Listen – I didn't say it would work, and any engineer would have a fit if they saw my washing machine, but it looks good in a dark corner of the scullery! The lid from the cotton buds container had the wonderful advantage of three recesses which were just right for setting the legs into. The balsa wood lid and small wheel wrenched from a toy lorry are almost right, and will have to do. The general impression is convincing!

## Method

1 Cut the cocktail stirrers, perm curlers or knitting needles to the right length for the legs and slot them into the recesses in the cotton buds container top. Spray the whole thing white with car spray paint.
2 Use the thin metal foil to make bands and stick them in place.

## Materials

*Plastic top from cotton buds container*
*Cocktail stirrers, perm curlers or knitting needles*
*Balsa wood*
*Wheel from toy*
*Necklace clasp*
*Metal foil, thin and stiff*
*Paper*
*Wire*
*Card*
*Split pin*
*Watch wheel*
*Part of necklace fastener*
*Broken bits of jewellery*
*Beads and bead caps*
*Narrow rod*

3  Cut the balsa wood to shape for the lid and score it as shown.
4  The mechanism on top consists of a strip of card, curved, with a hole at either end.
5  Place a small metal washer in the centre of the lid and pierce the centre of the strip of card. The split pin goes through the washer to attach the strip to the lid as shown.
6  The thin rod goes through the ends of the card and the top of the split pin with beads positioned as illustrated.
7  Make the winding handle from the toy wheel and the necklace fastener and slide it on to one end of the rod with the watch wheel between it and the card strip.
8  Cover the top of the split pin with the part of the necklace hook.
9  The wringer is made from two small rolls of paper placed between two balsa wood pieces.
10  Another strip of card goes over the top of the rollers.
11  The handle is a piece of wire, a bead cap and a bead.
12  Finally, the wringer is fixed in a tray made from stiff metal foil, and attached to the back of the washing machine.

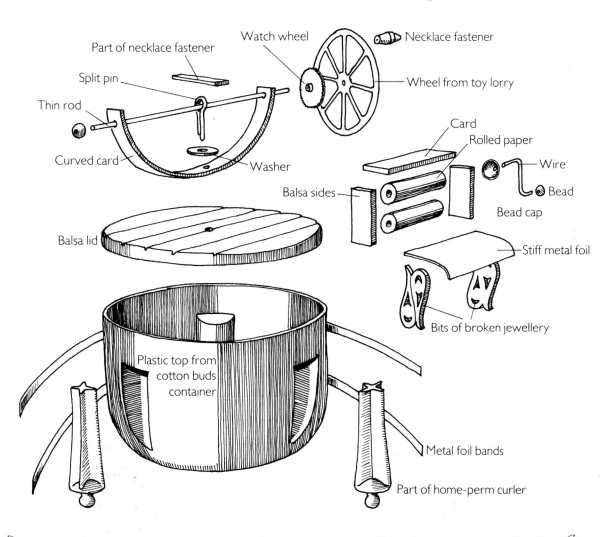

Part of necklace fastener

Watch wheel

Necklace fastener

Split pin

Wheel from toy lorry

Thin rod

Card

Rolled paper

Wire

Curved card

Washer

Bead

Bead cap

Balsa sides

Stiff metal foil

Balsa lid

Bits of broken jewellery

Plastic top from cotton buds container

Metal foil bands

Part of home-perm curler

## Materials

*Corrugated paper; thin card*
*Hairs from paintbrush; cocktail*
*   stick*
*Wooden serviette ring;*
*   card; foil*
*Pieces of plastic doyley, fine*
*   dowelling (from place mat)*

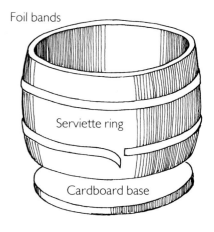

Foil bands

Serviette ring

Cardboard base

# Clothes Airer, Washboard, Tub and Broom

### Method

### Washboard
Use two pieces of card to make the frame. Add a small square of corrugated paper.

### Broom
Bend the paintbrush hairs over the end of the cocktail stick, glue and bind them.

### Tub
Make a card base for the serviette ring and bind the ring with two strips of foil.

### Clothes airer
Slot the tiny dowel rods through the pieces of plastic doyley.

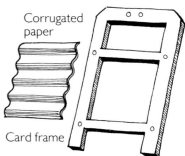

Corrugated paper

Card frame

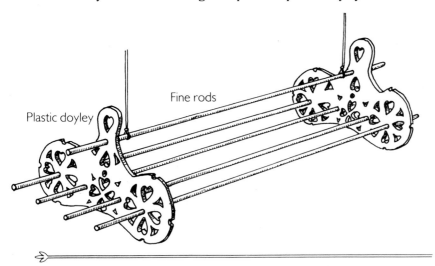

Fine rods

Plastic doyley

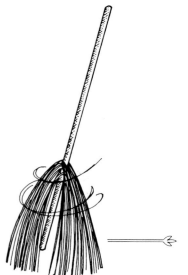

# THE SHOPS

# 13

# Ironmonger

*The lovely thing about all the shops is that their wares can be swapped with the rooms in the house to give endless permutations and new ideas. The Ironmonger's is great fun to furnish because in late Victorian and Edwardian times all kinds of odd and obscure labour-saving inventions were thought up. Most have faded into obscurity, but you can still create all sorts of objects and then decide what their functions might have been!*

# Balcony Balustrade

Well – this was another example of things that happen to turn up. I had decided that a balcony hung with hardware was required; this started with a plain rail, but when a filigree metal 'After Eight' tray presented itself at a jumble sale, I paid 10p for it and hoped it would be long enough when opened up to make a balustrade, also that it would come to pieces without my having to resort to violence. It did, although it wasn't quite long enough, so I had to cut it into three and put pillars in between. I painted it white before putting it in place, and it made marvellous wrought-iron railings.

## Method

1  Open up 'After Eight' tray (discard structural parts).
2  Cut filigree sides into three pieces.
3  Space with balsa-wood blocks.
4  Top blocks with beads.
5  Glue in place and paint.

## Materials

*'After Eight' display tray*
*½" × ½" balsa strip*
*Cotton balls or beads*

# Wooden Display Stand

Using balsa wood or card, you can make a variety of display stands to go inside your shop or out on the forecourt. I have filled mine with beads, but of course what you put in yours depends on the kind of shop you are making.

**Materials**

*Balsa wood or card*
*Odd beads*

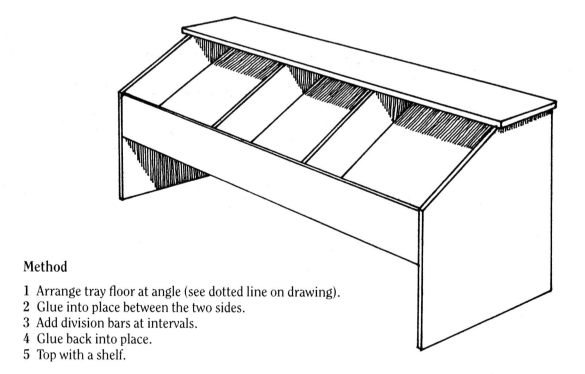

### Method

1 Arrange tray floor at angle (see dotted line on drawing).
2 Glue into place between the two sides.
3 Add division bars at intervals.
4 Glue back into place.
5 Top with a shelf.

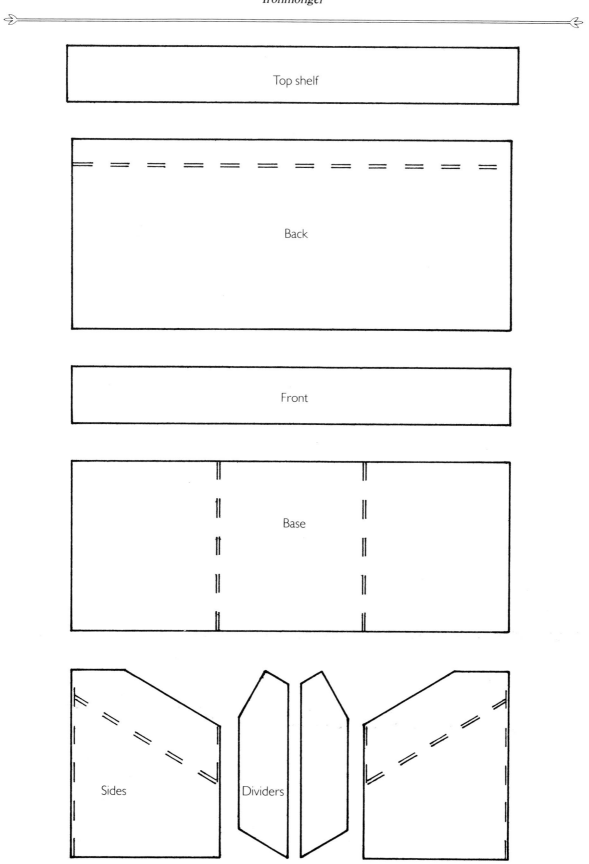

Top shelf

Back

Front

Base

Sides

Dividers

# Delivery Hand-cart

The Ironmonger's boasts a delivery service and employs the Cummin twins as delivery boys – Isambard (known as Izzie) and Willoughby Cummin. The unfortunate tradesmen who pulled these delivery carts may not have cherished them, but they seem quaint and nostalgic to us now. Surely there are many people still around who remember Wall's 'Stop Me and Buy One' tricycle carts, which were adaptations of the hand-cart. Two wheels wrenched off a broken toy lorry were the basis of my hand-cart, together with the springs from a railway-wagon kit. The rest was easy. I am proud to say that on seeing the resulting model several people have said, 'Ah, but it's a kit, isn't it!' High praise, I reckon.

## Method

1  Make side, ends, base and roof from card. Glue sides to ends to make box; add base.
2  Bend roof and glue in place.
3  Glue ridge to centre of roof.
4  Decorate ridge with necklace clasp.
5  Stick axles and wheels in place.
6  Glue scarf ring, face upwards, to underside of base.
7  Make up and glue handle and shaft.
8  Decorate base of shaft with broken jewellery.
9  Paint and letter with rub-on lettering.

*Note:* scarf ring can open or close, allowing hand-cart to stand or lean.

### Materials

*Two matching wheels and axle*
*Necklace clasp*
*Tee-square cocktail stick*
*Scarf ring*
*Forked pins*
*Card*
*Beads*
*Dry-print lettering*

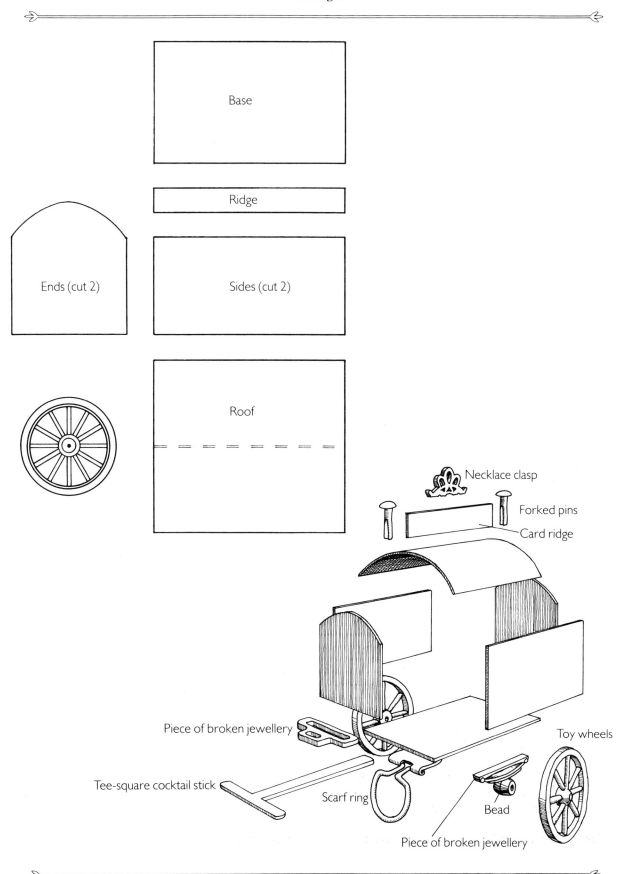

Base

Ridge

Ends (cut 2)

Sides (cut 2)

Roof

Necklace clasp

Forked pins

Card ridge

Piece of broken jewellery

Toy wheels

Tee-square cocktail stick

Scarf ring

Bead

Piece of broken jewellery

# Forecourt Display Items

I remember and love the complicated forecourt displays where it seemed that more than half the shop's goods were on the pavement outside (see page 112). I extended the base on which the shop stood so as to provide this area, crowding more wares on to the balcony. Of course this means there are more items to find or make, but as making things is my hobby this was no problem. I like the gleam of brass, so have a high proportion of metal objects both inside and outside the shop. Most of the stock is based on authentic household necessities of the time. I admit that some of these items are made up, but the ironmongery looks shiny and authentic when on display and I am delighted how often people fall upon some gadget I've invented, shrieking, 'My mum had one of these!', and proceed to tell me what it was used for.

Look for brass or copper cylinders, scent-bottle tops, lipstick tubes, heating-pipe joiners, cigar tubes and asthma inhalers. Use brass buttons, shaft uppermost, for lids with handles.

Sometimes the find will suggest its own use. I came across four large triangular metal beads; with buttons for lids they became teapots. Hooks (from hooks and eyes) made the handles and long beads formed the spouts.

## Materials

*Brass cylinders*
*Brass buttons with shafts*
*Flat brass buttons*
*Dress-stud*
*Metal washers*
*Earring clips*
*Watch winders*
*Belt-hole findings*
*Broken jewellery*
*Metal bottle-tops*

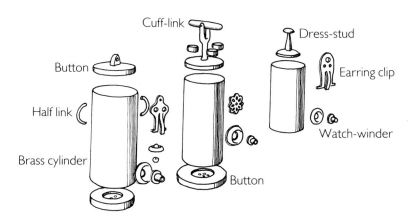

## Method

How these will turn out depends on the makings you use. I will tell you how to make one; then you can improvise. The real fun comes when you have to decide what function they perform.

1 Use metal scent-spray-top as cylinder.
2 Top with a metal button, shaft uppermost, as handle.
3 Use metal button as base.
4 Cut a chain link in half; use halves as handles.
5 Use washer and belt-hole rim as spout.
6 Decorate with an earring clip.

*Note:* pans on the right are metal bottle-tops with shaft buttons as lids.

# Outside Hanging Gas Lamps

Every turn-of-the-century shop worthy of its name had these monster lamps swinging precariously from brackets. I decided I absolutely must have a matching pair, and tried cutting a ping-pong ball in two, but it was impossible to keep it neat. Digging through my collection of useful bits, I came across the little plastic Kinder Eggs that contain toys; these were just a little larger than a Christmas-tree light-holder, so I put a curtain ring between the two and it made a perfect fit.

### Method

1 Use the top of a Kinder Egg shell for the lamp. Paint it white.
2 Fit lamp with a lid made from a button.
3 Glue fairy-light holder upside down to button or curtain ring.
4 Top with half a cuff-link or bead.
5 Fit open end of split pin into central hole and glue.
6 Add beads at bottom of lamp.
7 Thread crossbar through opening of split pin.
8 Hang chain from each end of crossbar.

*Note:* to attach lamp to front of shop, use a second split pin threaded through a cylinder, and then a washer. Top with a twiddly-bit (a necklace fastener or piece of broken jewellery serves very well).

### Materials

*Christmas-tree light-holder*
*Kinder Egg or plastic capsule*
*Cuff-links or half beads*
*Split pins*
*Chain with bead or 'jump' ring*
   *attached*
*Beads and bead caps*
*Long jewellery link*

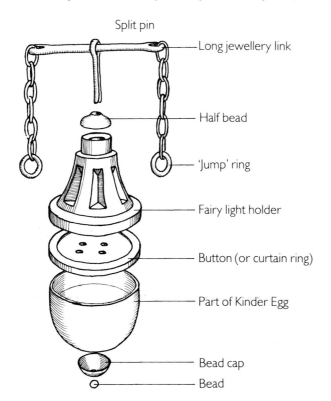

Split pin

Long jewellery link

Half bead

'Jump' ring

Fairy light holder

Button (or curtain ring)

Part of Kinder Egg

Bead cap

Bead

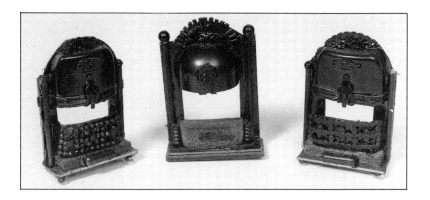

# Cast-iron Fireplaces

There were endless varieties of these little beauties from 1850 onwards, and more than most things they give a date to a room and set the tone. They can stand free or be built into an existing fireplace in your dolls' house, or be on display for sale in your shop. I was starting from scratch and set out to make six, all different, in the same evening. They were easy to make, cost next to nothing, look convincing and incidentally make very good presents for fellow dolls' house enthusiasts, who are usually delighted when told that the main makings were a sweetener dispenser or part of a Kinder Egg. Next time you take the children out to the shops, remember that the little treat you buy them may well end up as a handsome fireplace for you!

**Materials**

*Sweetener dispenser, or plastic
    pill-bottle
Part of Kinder Egg
Broken jewellery
Earring clip
Plastic doyley
Card and beads*

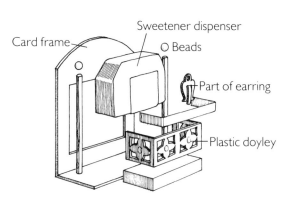

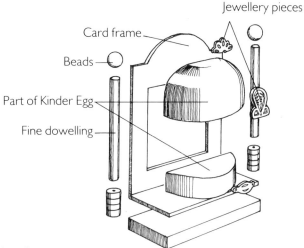

## Method

1 Cut out background frame in card. Remove central arch.
2 Score and bend base part forward, for hearth.
3 Cut Kinder Egg or sweetener dispenser to make hood.
4 Use lower piece of egg (or dispenser) to make grate.
5 Glue in place on card.
6 Add uprights on either side.
7 Decorate with broken jewellery or pieces of plastic doyley.
8 Paint black or dark grey.

# Bucketful of Brooms

To make brooms I used an old pasting-brush (though any brush that has bristles set in a row will do for this method). I cut a groove along a piece of balsa wood, applied glue to the groove, then straddled it along a line of bristles. When the glue dried I was able to cut the bristles free from the pasting-brush. Then I cut my new broom into short lengths and gave each a handle made from a cocktail stick. Finally I arranged them all in a bucket made from a shampoo bottle-top to which I added a handle of thin wire.

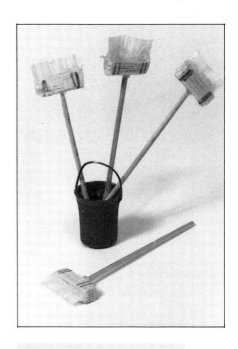

### Method

1 Cut groove horizontally along a piece of strip wood.
2 Straddle a line of brush-tufts into this groove.
3 Glue into place.
4 When firmly stuck, cut line of bristles away from mother brush.
5 Cut new broom into short lengths.
6 Fit each broom with a cocktail-stick handle.
7 Fit wire handle to cream container. Place brooms in bucket.

### Materials

*Bristles in a row*
*Balsa-wood strip*
*Cocktail sticks*
*Plastic bottle-top*
*Wire*

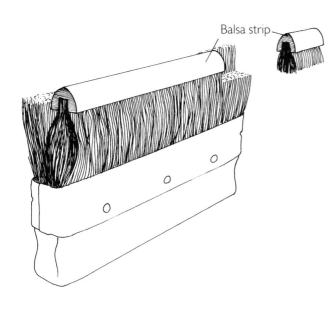

Balsa strip

Cocktail stick

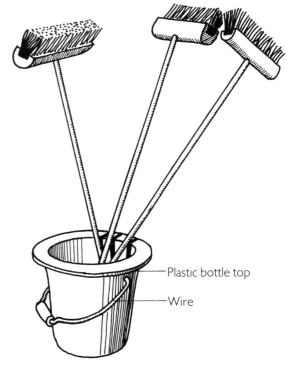

Plastic bottle top

Wire

# Washing-up Bowls

When you go out to tea, try to choose a café where they give you individual jam portions in a foil tub. Enhanced with handles made from eyes (from hooks and eyes), they make convincing washing-up bowls.

# Mangle

Even the youngest people seem to know what a mangle was, and when I show my dolls' house makes it's this well-named 'finger-crusher' that seems to evoke the most memories and remind them of visits to Gran's or encounters with the dreaded thing. Probably half the women who were in service had one extra-long finger resulting from an argument with a mangle!

I have made mangles both for my dolls' house and to stand on the forecourt of the ironmonger's shop.

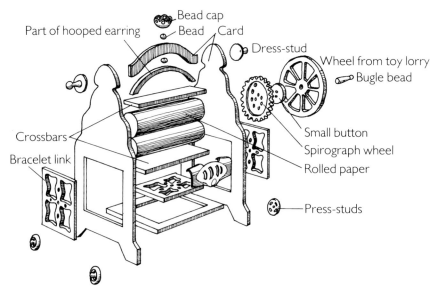

**Materials**

*Card for sides*
*Paper or tube*
*Bracelet links*
*Hoop earrings*
*Spirograph cogged wheels*
*Wheel from model lorry*
*Press-studs, dress-studs, bead caps, broken bits of jewellery*

## Method

1 Cut two side panels from card.
2 Cut out squares from the panels.
3 Glue filigreed links over squares.
4 Frame third link and cut it into a crossbar.
5 Make two more crossbars (plain) the same size.
6 Cut strip of typing paper to the same width. Place filigreed crossbar between sides as a tray and glue in place.
7 Glue second crossbar to form mangle base.
8 Roll the strip of paper into two cylinders; glue one above the other for rollers.
9 Top with third crossbar.
10 Unbend a hoop earring and glue above third crossbar.
11 Cut top spring from card; glue in place.
12 Top with bead cap on a bead, or a glue-tube piercer.
13 Glue dress-studs on outsides of side pieces.
14 Glue cogged Spirograph wheel in place.
15 Glue small button in centre of Spirograph wheel.
16 Glue wheel to button and finish with a handle made from a bugle bead.
17 Decorate front with bead cap or fancy piece of jewellery.
18 Add press-studs as feet.
19 Paint.

# Oil Lamps

A variety of these can be made, but how they will look depends on what bits of jewellery you can find. Look for necklaces which have bead caps between the beads: these are lovely filigreed cups which are endlessly useful in modelling. Once you have the makings, simply pile one part on another, using a pin in the centre to keep the finished lamp from leaning. I illustrate one of my favourite lamps to show you how to start. (See also page 47).

## Method

1 Choose base – button or earring minus central stone.
2 Glue large bead to base.
3 Insert needle (to be removed later), to keep things centred.
4 Add bead spacer or tiny bell.
5 Glue bead cap in place.
6 Add large pearl for lamp.
7 Top with small bead cap or a cut from a clear drinking straw for funnel.
8 Thread a gold bead on a pin and pierce bead spacer.
9 Thread on a bugle bead and a bead cap.
10 Cut off pin and take out the upright stabilizing needle.

### Materials

*Earring (without central stone)*
*Bead and bead caps*
*Metal bead spacer*
*Bugle and gold beads*
*Pearl bead*
*Needle*
*Pin*

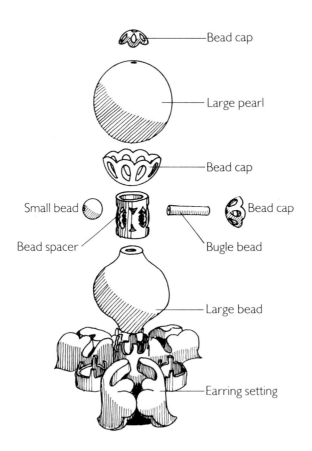

Bead cap

Large pearl

Bead cap

Small bead

Bead spacer

Bugle bead

Bead cap

Large bead

Earring setting

# Ironmonger's Scales

Do you remember when nails were sold by the pound and ironmonger's scales had a scoop which acted as a weighing tray?

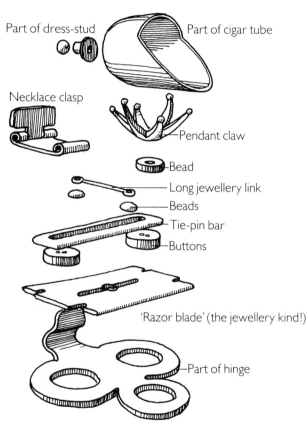

Part of dress-stud

Part of cigar tube

Necklace clasp

Pendant claw

Bead

Long jewellery link

Beads

Tie-pin bar

Buttons

'Razor blade' (the jewellery kind!)

Part of hinge

## Materials

*Fancy razor-blade (the fake kind that 'medallion man' used to wear)*
*Door-hinge or similar for base*
*Cigar tube*
*Necklace clasps, various*
*Pendant claw*
*Tiepin bar*
*Flat gold beads*
*Buttons*
*Part of dress-stud*

## Method

1 Glue fancy razor-blade to hinge or base.
2 Mount tiepin bar on two small buttons.
3 Glue to razor-blade.
4 Cross the centre of bar with link mounted on two beads.
5 Cut rounded end of cigar tube to shape for scoop.
6 Glue dress-stud handle to rounded end of scoop.
7 Mount scoop on a pendant claw on top of a flat bead on one end of tiepin bar.
8 Glue necklace clasp to other end.

# Kitchen Gadgets

Beg or borrow a copy of Mrs Beeton's *Household Management* some time and set yourself to make some kitchen gadgets in miniature. Does your kitchen or ironmonger's boast a duck press, a mincer, coffee grinder or sausage extruder? Shame on you – go forth and make one!

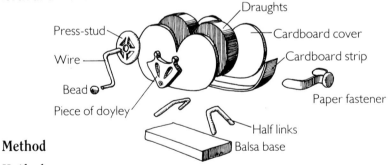

## Materials

**Knife sharpener**
*Two draughts counters*
*Plastic doyley*
*Necklace links*
*Necklace fasteners*
*Brass paper fastener*
*Wire and bead*
*Balsa wood and card*

## Method

### Knife sharpener

1 Place draughts side by side on lightweight card and draw round them.
2 Cut card to the shape shown to cover them.
3 Cut and glue strip inset to complete the cover. Glue to make box.
4 Insert draughts into cover.
5 Mount on to base, using two half chain-links.
6 Open up a paper fastener to look like John Wayne's legs.
7 Fit paper fastener as handle.
8 Decorate with broken jewellery or bits of doyley.
9 Add handle made from bent wire and bead.

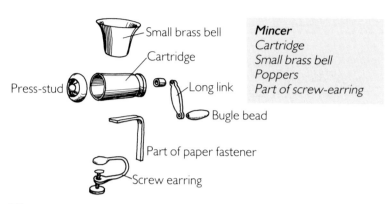

*Mincer*
*Cartridge*
*Small brass bell*
*Poppers*
*Part of screw-earring*

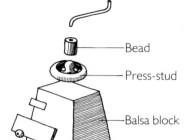

## Mincer
1 Glue press-stud to closed end of cartridge.
2 Bend wire for handle; glue bead to one end and attach the other end to half a necklace clasp. Glue to open end of cartridge.
3 Attach bell to top.
4 Add small piece of bent wire to bottom of cartridge.
5 Glue earring finding below. The great advantage of this is that you can really clamp the mincer to your dolls' house table.

*Coffee grinder*
*Balsa-wood block*
*Part of jewellery*
*Popper*
*Wire*

## Coffee grinder
1 Cut balsa-wood block to box shape.
2 Glue on four beads as feet.
3 Top with a press-stud.
4 Shape wire handle, thread bead on one end of knob.
5 Glue wire into half a necklace clasp and attach to press-stud.

## Duck press
1 Glue a small spring from a pen in the centre of a key-hanger.
2 Top key-hanger with small beads on either side of one large one.
3 Add spout – half a necklace clasp on a washer.

## Sausage extruder
1 Cut large felt-pen top down to size.
2 Top with a small bell.
3 To the front, glue small felt-pen top.
4 To the back, glue a small section of felt pen.
5 Add a press-stud.
6 Attach handle of bent wire, with bead as knob.

*Duck press*
*Plastic bottle-top*
*Scout's belt key-hanger*
*Press-stud*
*Half necklace clasp*
*Spring from ballpoint pen*

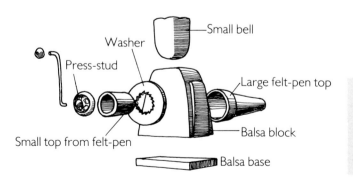

*Sausage extruder*
*Top from large felt marker pen*
*Small bell or cup*
*Felt-pen top and press-stud*
*Watch winder*
*Wire and bead*

# Drip-feed Oil Stove

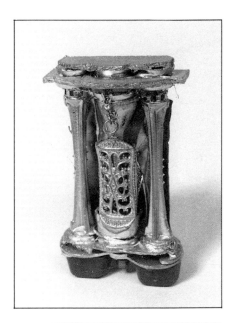

I fell in love with a picture of this stove, so without much understanding of how it works I set about making a scale model. Using card for a shield, I mounted it on two plastic washers, making the pillars out of home-perm curlers which went on either side of a rectangular bracelet link stuck to a golf tee. The top was made of two layers of shaped card with washers between. The trick of uniting all these separate, disparate items is to spray the finished model in one colour, in this case grey.

### Materials

*Home-perm curlers*
*Golf tee*
*Washers*
*Metal bracelet link*
*Card*

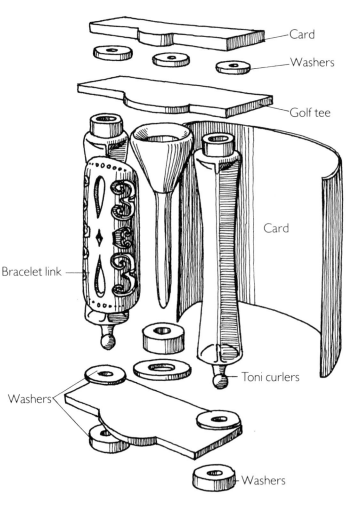

Card
Washers
Golf tee
Card
Bracelet link
Toni curlers
Washers
Washers

### Method

1 Cut three identical card pieces to use as base, shelf and lid.
2 Mount base on two washers as feet.
3 Glue three washers in line on base.
4 Stand golf tee on end in centre washer; glue.
5 Glue home-perm curler stalks into flanking washers.
6 Back with light card.
7 Mask golf tee with elaborate filigree link.
8 Glue shelf in place.
9 Mount three washers side by side on shelf.
10 Glue lid in place.
11 Paint black or grey; the original was orange.

# 14

# Pawnbroker

*This shop is more modern, dated about 1918, and is made from a kit I bought at a dolls' house show. I constructed it by following the basic instructions and then adapted it, aiming once again for the cluttered look so typical of old shops.*

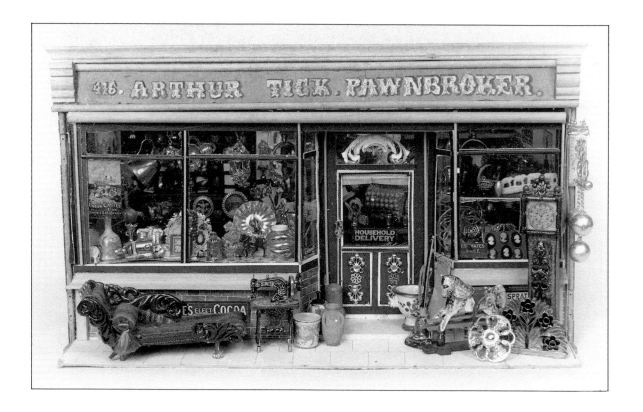

Of course, the nice thing about choosing to model a pawnbroker's shop is that, again, it can house things you have both made and bought. Friends and family often give me miniature knick-knacks – and what am I to do with them, since my boast is that I make everything myself out of rubbish? So this shop was made up with the idea of displaying my miniatures – made, bought and given.

The shop is in the suburbs and Arthur – a mild-mannered man with a permanent cold, who was unfit for service in the First World War due to everything from poor eyesight to flat feet – lives above the shop with his wife Polly (who is a suffragette), and his children Anne and Fran (short for Frances). His brother, who works as a waiter in the evenings, often helps out during the day (Waiter Tick).

# Interior Shop Fittings

D IY shops yield plenty of goods with modelling potential. They
also sell stick-on gilded mouldings for furniture, which are
very useful to the modeller. I have used these as mirror frames,
door mantels and even bath ends. Finding it hard to make up
pigeonholes and keep them in an exact grid, I used tile-spacers
taken straight from the packet before being broken into little
crosses. Mirrored plastic sheet can be bought from hobby shops
and cut to shape using scissors. Frame with adhesive trimmings.
See pages 26, 27 and 47 for picture framing, trophies and lamps.

## Materials

**Mirrors**
*Handbag mirror*
*Gilded mouldings*

**Pigeonholes**
*Tiling spacers*
*Card or balsa strips*

Card or balsa shelves and back

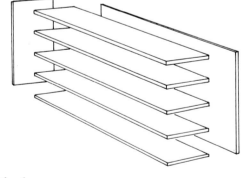

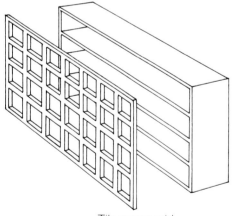

Tile spacer grid

## Method

1 Cut card to fit tile-spacer grid.
2 Cut shelves to fit.
3 Cut two unit ends.
4 Fit shelves and unit ends to back.
5 Face with tile-spacer grid.
6 Build up ends with turned sticks.
7 Fill pigeonholes with odd beads, bead caps and paper.

# Cake Dishes, Bowls, Powder Bowls

You can never have too many of these in a pawnshop or in your dolls' house, and they can be made in minutes. They are easy for children to invent and make nice presents for other dolls'-house enthusiasts. Look out for blouses in jumble sales, just for their useful glass buttons! See also page 35.

**Materials**

*Glass or plastic buttons*
*Glass or plastic beads*
*Filigree bead caps*
*Collar-studs*
*Flat gold buttons*

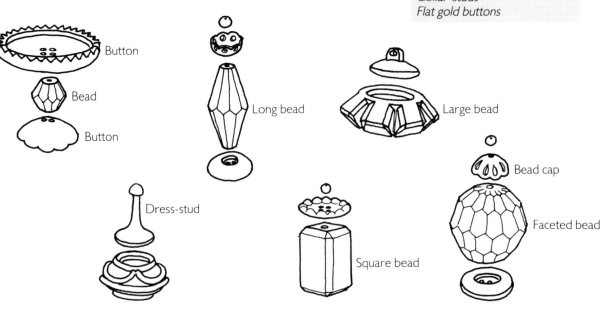

# Fire-screens

I'm sure that by now you have collected lots of brooches and similar things from jumble sales.

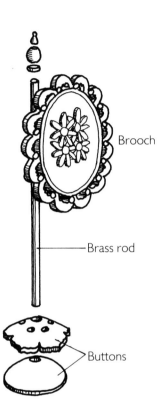

Brooch

Brass rod

Buttons

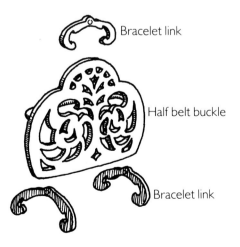

Bracelet link

Half belt buckle

Bracelet link

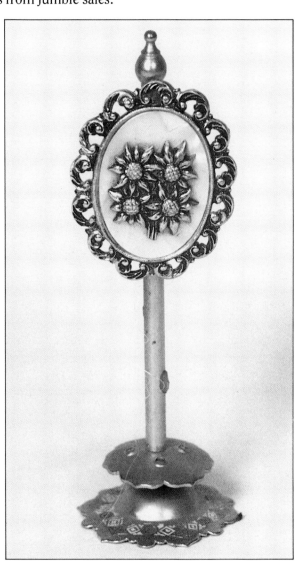

## Materials

**Upright firescreen**
Scarf ring
Brass rod
Buttons and bead

**Low screen**
Half nurse's belt buckle
Half link from a bracelet
    (for handle and each foot)

# Oil-powered Magic Lantern

This magic lantern used to stand in Major Rhodeahead's trophy room. I can only suppose that its fall from grace came about after the Memsahib – on one of her rare trips downstairs at 2 Chipsand Place – found what the Major was showing on it. No slides are in evidence, but rumour has it that some of the ladies on the slides in the Major's collection so far forgot themselves as to flaunt their ankles!

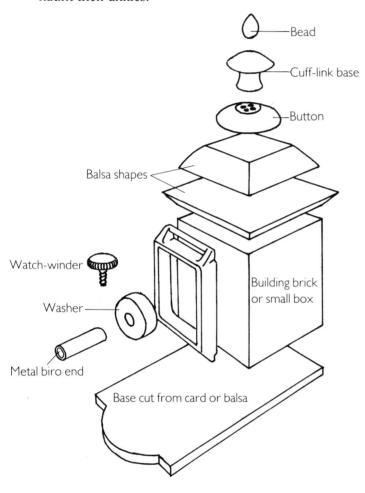

Bead

Cuff-link base

Button

Balsa shapes

Watch-winder

Washer

Metal biro end

Building brick or small box

Base cut from card or balsa

## Method

1 Make or find small box.
2 Cut base to size from card or balsa and glue box on to it.
3 Mount watch-face frame on box front.
4 Make projector lens from washer, metal Biro end and watch winder.
5 Top box with shaped balsa pieces.
6 Glue button on to balsa shape.
7 Add cuff-link base and bead.

## Materials

*Child's building brick or
   small box
Cuff-link base
Biro pen end
Card
Watch winder
Square watch-face surround
Bead
Button*

# Bust on Stand

Well-meaning people often give me items for my dolls' houses and I like to use them, but feel that it's cheating just to have them in their original form. Finding I had a Cluedo candlestick, I mounted it on a brooch, topped it with a small fancy button, and on that I glued a metal drawer handle. The bust of the Mem's father, General Strike, was made out of Fymo (see page 172), using a gold button as its base.

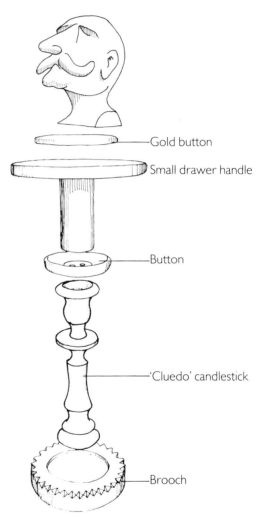

Gold button

Small drawer handle

Button

'Cluedo' candlestick

Brooch

## Method

1 Make or find statue (charms are good for this).
2 Mount on a button; spray gold.
3 Glue drawer handle to small button.
4 Make shaft from Cluedo candlestick.
5 Glue to base (brooch or draughts counter).
6 Spray brown.
7 Glue statue, mounted on button, on top.

## Materials

*Fymo bust on button*
*Small drawer handle*
*Buttons*
*Cluedo candlestick*
*Brooch with stone removed*

# Dressing Mirror

Can you cut glass? If so, this is for you, because you will need half a handbag mirror. Take the piece that survives, and you're off!

Method

1 Cut fancy buckle in half.
2 Glue halves on either side of whole buckle to make legs.
3 Attach tea-stirrers either side of mirror.
4 Glue mirror on to base.
5 Add decorations and paint.

## Materials

*Half small mirror*
*Two plastic tea-stirrers*
  *(courtesy BR)*
*Two fancy buckles*
*Beads*
*Card*
*Necklace clasp and bead caps*

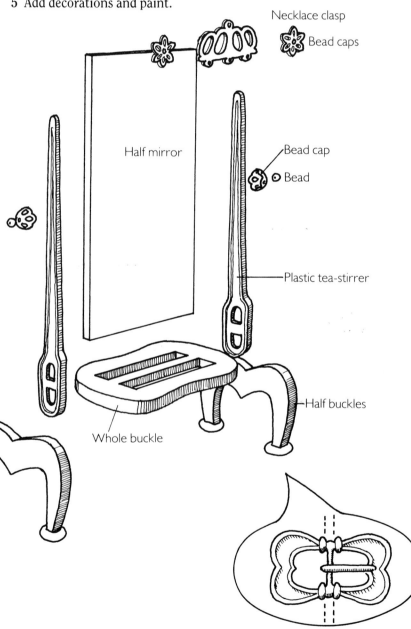

Necklace clasp

Bead caps

Half mirror

Bead cap

Bead

Plastic tea-stirrer

Half buckles

Whole buckle

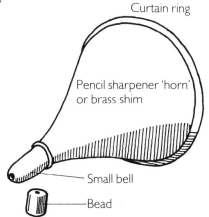

# Gramophone

This is not meant to work, but as long as you don't look too closely it's quite convincing! If you are lucky enough to find the horn part of a pencil-sharpener, it helps, but you can make a horn out of brass shim. Save the foil seal from a tin of coffee. This is not for the timid, but the results are well worth the perseverance.

## Method

If you are making a horn, cut out a foil quarter-circle and curl round to make a dunce's cap. Glue and attach curtain ring to rim, and small bell to the sharp end. If you've got this far, you are a candidate for making the gramophone itself.

1  Cut card a little larger than brick for top and base.
2  Glue above and below brick.
3  Cut a length from felt pen and glue side by side with 2·2 cartridge; the felt pen rests on a balsa shape with a concave surface.
4  Mount necklace clasps on to box top.
5  Thread paper fasteners through clasps and into ends of tube.
6  Mount horn on top of back tube, to overhang front tube. It is supported by the bead.
7  Fix press-stud for horn head.
8  Glue on handle assembly made from beads and wire.
9  Flatten large bead cap and use halves to decorate gramophone box, or use bits of broken jewellery.

## Materials

*Pencil-sharpener horn, or foil shim and curtain ring*
*Small bell*
*Tube from felt pen*
*2.2 cartridge*
*Press-studs*
*Balsa*
*Card*
*Brass paper fastener*
*Heavy hooks and eyes*
*Child's play brick*
*Wire, bead cap and bead*

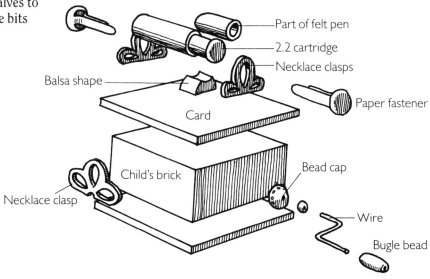

Curtain ring

Pencil sharpener 'horn' or brass shim

Press-stud

Small bell

Bead

Balsa shape

Part of felt pen

2.2 cartridge

Necklace clasps

Paper fastener

Card

Child's brick

Bead cap

Necklace clasp

Wire

Bugle bead

# Clocks

Clocks can vary from the very simple to the complicated, depending on what you have as makings. Clock faces can easily be cut from catalogues and mounted on buttons, or just use faces from broken watches. Earring settings, scarf rings, brooches or buckles can all become clock frames, and odd bits of filigree and animal 'charms' can give a wonderful 'Empire' effect. The clocks in the photograph and drawings are only a few examples of the many possibilities.

## Method

A This can be made in seconds. Stick the clock face to the button and use the scarf ring to frame it. It can then be mounted on another button for a base if you like.

### Materials

**A**
*Clock face*
*Button*
*Scarf ring*
*Bracelet link*

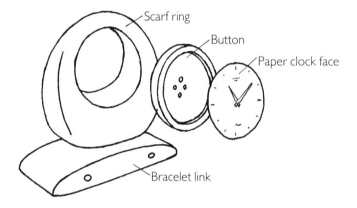

B The living-room clock is under a glass dome. Use the earring setting to frame the face and mount it on the dress clip. Use the button as a base and the cut-down test tube for the glass dome.

**B**
*Earring setting*
*Dress clip*
*Clock face*
*Buttons*
*Test tube*

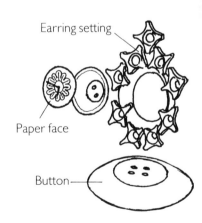

Earring setting

Paper face

Button

Section of test tube

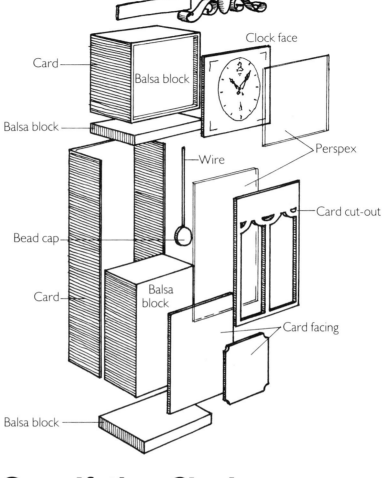

# Grandfather Clock

A grandfather clock is an absolute must for the hall. Many of the bought ones are awful so go ahead and make your own.

### Materials

*Balsa wood blocks*
*Stiff card, either already*
*   coloured brown or spray*
*   painted before you begin*
*Clear plastic or perspex*
*Picture of clock face*
*Bead caps*
*Wire*

### Method

1 Make up top and base as two separate boxes by wrapping card round back and sides of balsa wood blocks, leaving the fronts open.
2 Put the clock face in front of top box and cover with plastic or perspex.
3 Make pendulum from a piece of wire with a bead cap on the end.
4 Attach the end of the wire to the underside of the top box or the balsa layer beneath.
5 Add a plastic or perspex front.
6 Create the decorative and panelled effects with cardboard cutouts.
7 The clock can be made more elaborate by adding a base made from a block of balsa, for example, and bands etc.

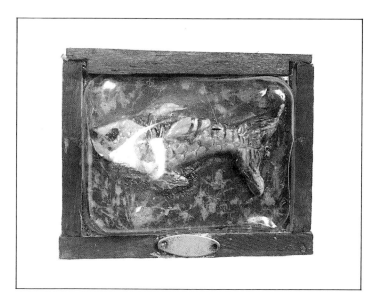

# Mounted Stuffed Fish

**K**eep an eye out for bubble packs, which come in all shapes and sizes and can be used for all kinds of things in miniature. This one held screws, and I simply put a fish in it and a frame round it.

### Materials

*Bubble pack*
*Fymo or salt dough*
*Bead for eye*
*Card for mounting*
*Balsa wood for frame*
*Tiny link for name-plate*

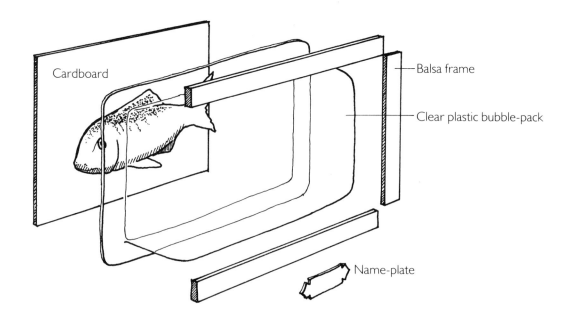

Cardboard

Balsa frame

Clear plastic bubble-pack

Name-plate

# Exercise Horse

This horse – one owner, officer and gentleman, in good condition (horse rather than owner) – was used by the Major who, wearing jodhpurs, took regular exercise on it. Even the Memsahib has been seen to use it, wearing full riding dress and riding side-saddle of course.

The Major has become more sedentary now and the Mem has taken to her bed with a glass of port – which, I suppose, is why the article has found its way to Arthur Tick's establishment. Believe it or not, this is an authentic model.

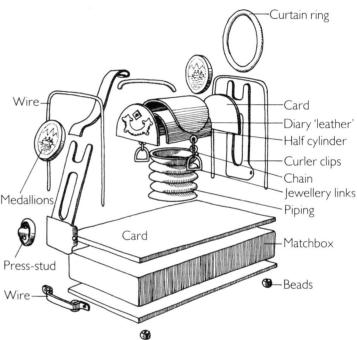

## Method

1 Cut card base and top to fit matchbox; glue in place.
2 Make up seat from half of cylinder; glue on semicircular card ends.
3 Mount seat on section of concertina piping.
4 Glue saddle (cut from diary cover) in place.
5 Add stirrups.
6 Curve two pieces of wire and glue in place for 'hold rails', front and back.
7 Glue a half curler clip in the centre of each wire.
8 Add medallion to back wire and curtain ring to top.
9 Add handlebar to front wire.
10 Decorate front wire with snap fastener and medallion.
11 Mount horse on four bead feet.
12 Glue handle to box front and link to saddle front.

### Materials

Card
Matchbox for base
Two curler clips
Concertina piping
Medallions or coins
Diary cover
Jewellery bits
Small cylinder
Wire
Curtain ring
Beads

# Cash Register

Sooner or later you will need a cash register if you are interested in modelling shops. The ornate Victorian variety can be made quite easily, although you will need a good picture to work from.

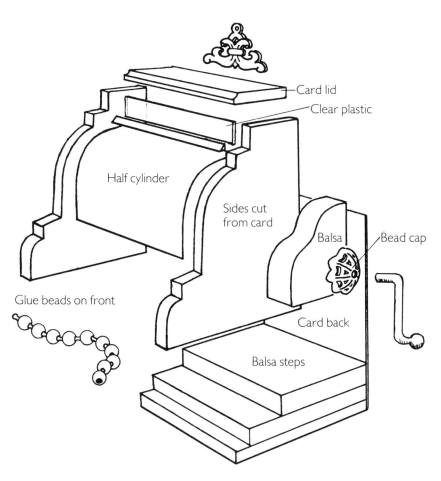

Card lid

Clear plastic

Half cylinder

Sides cut from card

Balsa

Bead cap

Glue beads on front

Card back

Balsa steps

## Method

*Note:* cover each stage in gold embossed paper as you make it.

 1  Cut back from firm card.
 2  Add three steps of balsa wood for base and drawer.
 3  Cut cylinder in half (you will use only one half).
 4  Mount cylinder above 'steps'.
 5  Cut two sides; glue in place.
 6  Insert clear plastic window.
 7  Finish with card shelf or lid.
 8  Top with 3-strand necklace clasp.
 9  Glue three rows of beads in place for keys.
10  Cut balsa-wood handle unit for side; glue.
11  Add bent wire handle through a bead cap. Glue.

## Materials

*Card or balsa wood*
*Small cylinder*
*Rows of white plastic beads*
*Clear plastic*
*Necklace clasp*
*Gold embossed cake-frill*

# Treadle Sewing Machine

## Materials

### Base
Links from metal filigree
   bracelet
Buckle
Paper fasteners

### Machine
Balsa wood
Paper
Cuff-link
Watch wheel
Curtain ring
Beads
Necklace fastening
Pin
Brooch
Bead caps squashed flat

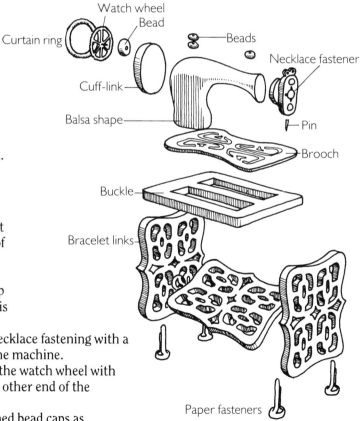

## Method

### Base
1 The three bracelet links form the sides and treadle of the machine.
2 Put a paper fastener at each corner as a foot.
3 The buckle is the table of the base.

### Machine
1 Cut the basic machine shape from balsa. (When I first tried this I broke the balsa, but sandwiched the pieces between two pieces of paper to retrieve the situation.)
2 The exploded diagram shows all the components in place. The brooch sits on top of the buckle, and the balsa machine shape is placed on top of that.
3 The sewing mechanism is made from the necklace fastening with a pin inserted into it and fixed to the end of the machine.
4 The cuff-link followed by another bead and the watch wheel with the tiny curtain ring as trim are fixed at the other end of the machine.
5 Use more beads to finish off top, and squashed bead caps as decoration for the sides.

# 15

# Fish and Game Shop

*This is a small lock-up shop. The display slab would be hosed down at the end of the day, so there is a gutter at its base. Then the slab would be pushed inside the shop and the roller-blind pulled down and padlocked. This makes modelling particularly easy.*

# Styling the Shop

I used a three-sided box with extended base and a clear plastic lid to allow light into the shop. The fascia is built up high to conceal the roof (see page 17). The floor is covered in Contact self-adhesive plastic, the blind is made from a split bamboo table mat, and bridge girders from a model railway kit are used above the window to complete the effect.

Below is a list of the materials I used to make the Display of Fish and Slab, Gutter and Cover, and Dustbin and Hosepipe.

### Method

**Display of Fish and Slab**

The display stand is made from card and balsa, but I have discovered that polystyrene from meat-trays looks like marble, so I topped my stand with this and used it for the display divisions, and even the shop step and forecourt floor.

The display of fish (and poultry) is made from salt dough (see page 147 for recipe) baked, coloured and varnished. Some people use proprietary modelling clays, but these are expensive and tend to be rather highly coloured.

## Materials

### *Display of Fish and Slab*
*Stiff card*
*Balsa*
*Textured polystyrene meat-tray*
*Salt dough*

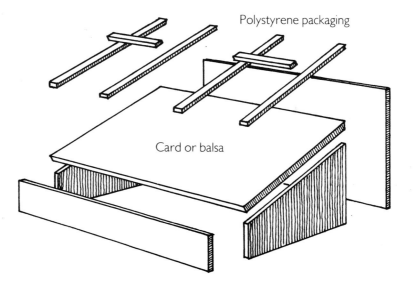

Polystyrene packaging

Card or balsa

### Gutter and Cover

To avoid cutting a groove in my base-board, I created the channel by building up the pavement instead. I used a polystyrene meat-tray with a convenient diamond pattern on it, then I covered the gutter with a grid cut from sieve-mesh. A fancy bracelet link formed the drain cover.

### *Gutter and Cover*
*Textured polystyrene meat-tray*
*Sieve-mesh*
*Bracelet link*

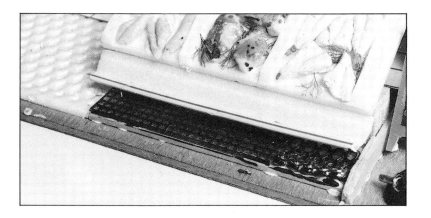

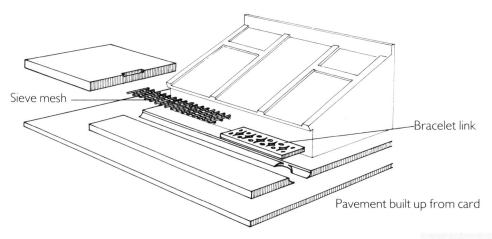

Sieve mesh

Bracelet link

Pavement built up from card

### Dustbin
The film container has the large button as a lid and the 'eye' from the hook and eye is the handle.

### Hosepipe
The necklace fastener forms the nozzle and connector of the hosepipe, which is made from the bell-flex.

***Dustbin***
*35mm film container*
*Large button with shaft*
*Eyes from hooks and eyes*

***Hosepipe***
*Length of bell-flex*
*Screw-type necklace fastener*

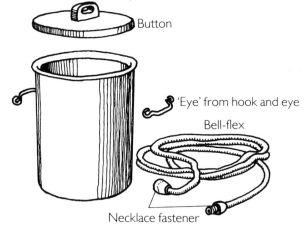

Button

'Eye' from hook and eye

Bell-flex

Necklace fastener

# Telephone in Pay Kiosk

Though the shop is poky, there is a small pay booth where Millie Pede is always ready to lend a hand. This has a telephone and a spike for bills. The dead-fish pictures were reduced on a photocopier from old recipe books and coloured by hand.

### Method

1 Use button as base.
2 Glue end of mapping-pen upright for stem.
3 Mount belt-hole liner at angle for mouthpiece.
4 Make earphone rest out of wire wrapped round stem.
5 Glue press-stud in place for dial.
6 Cut candle-holder to make ear-piece.
7 Top with tiny bead cap through which you have threaded cotton.
8 Attach cotton to base.
9 The bill spike is simply an upturned drawing pin with squares of paper impaled on it.

### Materials

*Button*
*Top of mapping-pen*
*Press-stud*
*Belt-hole liner*
*Sewing cotton*
*Cake candle-holder*
*Wire*
*Bead cap*
*Drawing pin*

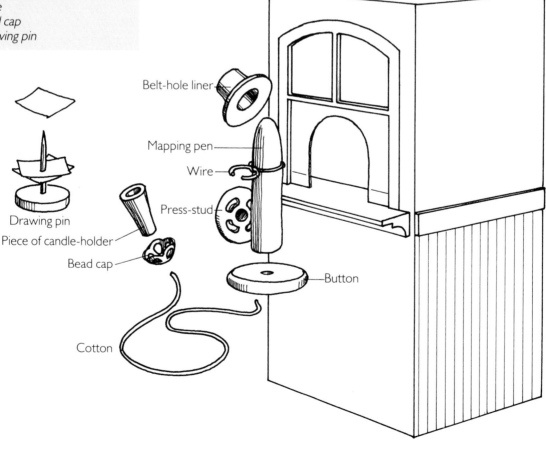

# Interior Gas Lamp

Start by cutting a test tube – no easy matter. I used a triangular file; having filed a neat line all round the tube, I gave it a decisive tap and it promptly shattered to smithereens! Practice makes adequate, if not perfect. After that it's easy.

## Method

This is a pile-up job, and to prevent it from taking a list to starboard I recommend you thread all the parts on to a central needle, which you can either cut to size or remove entirely when the glue has dried.

### Materials

*End of a test tube*
*Plastic ring*
*Bead caps*
*Earrings minus centre*
*Gold button*
*Cap of felt-pen*
*Metal rod*
*Split pin and chain*

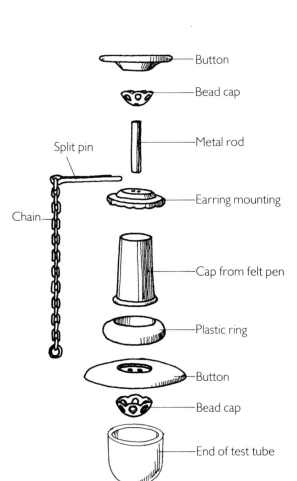

- Button
- Bead cap
- Metal rod
- Split pin
- Chain
- Earring mounting
- Cap from felt pen
- Plastic ring
- Button
- Bead cap
- End of test tube

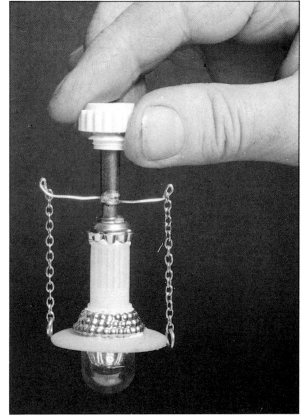

Upstairs in the bakers . . . with business going on down below.

The bakers shop in full.

The ironmongers offers dozens of opportunities for making original miniatures.

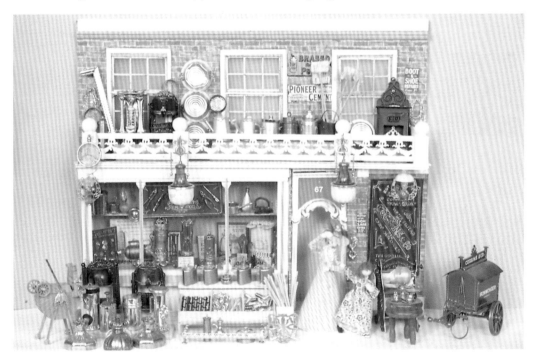

The pawnbroker has a particularly turn-of-the-century atmosphere.

Inside the pawnbroker – note the big shiny cash register!

*Below left* Pigeonholes contain all kinds of goodies.

More fascinating clutter from Arthur Tick.

The fish and game shop with an abundant display of wares.

Many potent potions in the window of the chemist . . .

. . . and many more potions inside.

The photographer has a particularly discreet and restrained exterior.

Part of the fun is creating an overall effect and atmosphere, as has been achieved in this delightful scene at the photographers.

Just a sample of the hundreds of different odds and ends from which the pieces in this book can be made.

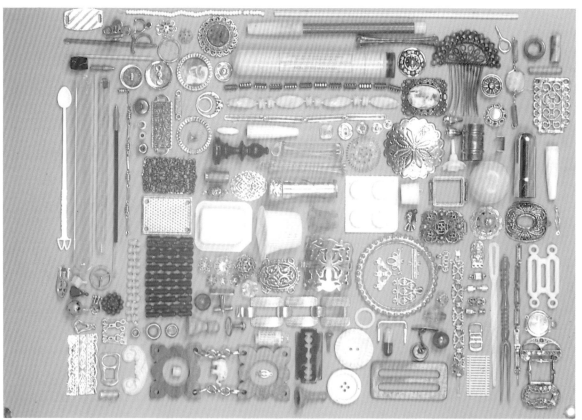

# 16

# Baker

*At first the baker's had no name on the front. It
belonged to a kindly, dumpy lady called Megan Rees,
who managed alone for some years until just before
the First World War when she married Karl
Schuffelmeyer, a master-baker who was visiting her
village in Wales.*

# Making a Roof

The quality of the confectionery improved enormously in the little shop, but because they had to pay the signwriter by the letter – and also because of certain anti-German feelings in the village – he took his wife's name by deed poll and the name Karl O. Rees appears on the fascia. The fact that I was dieting at the time has nothing to do with the sound of it!

To make the baker's shop I first made a mock-up of what I wanted in light card; then when I was sure of the measurements of the individual pieces I took the templates to my local DIY store and they cut hardboard to the sizes I required. As I am no expert in making dolls' houses – my main interest being to furnish and decorate them – all I will offer is my method of making a roof that looks convincing. I did this by scoring the horizontal lines on a piece of card which was large enough to be folded in the centre and thus make the whole roof. I scored the perpendicular tile lines and carefully lifted them at the base. When I put the card in place over the existing roof I painted it, picking out odd tiles in another tone of the terra cotta colour, and finished the whole thing with a bent and scored ridge-tile. Once the roof was varnished some tiles tightened and lifted a little, giving a pleasing patchy effect.

Windows are important, and I like to make mine from Flexiglass which does not distort. I made shelves and dressed the window first. Brick-paper gave the wall a good finish, decorated here and there with commercial scale adverts.

# Salt Dough Pastry

**Recipe**

*4 cups plain flour*
*1 cup salt*
*1 tsp cooking oil*
*Water to mix (to consistency*
*of pastry)*

You will find that you can roll this and cut out shapes with small cylinders (use a lipstick top for cake size). The added oil gives the pastry elasticity, so you can pull it about and also incorporate wire, cotton, etc. – enabling you to make strings of sausages and the like. Try topping tiny individual cakes with a red bead for a cherry, pushed in before baking.

Bake as normal pastry for about 15 minutes (until light brown). Paint with watercolours and then varnish (don't forget to wash the varnish brush after use in turps or white spirit). Use buttons as plates. (An alternative recipe is given on page 91.)

# Pot-bellied Stove

I needed two pot-bellied stoves, and being unable to find realistic commercially made ones, decided to create my own. One was for the baker's shop (upstairs) and the other to gleam darkly in a corner of my dolls' house scullery. I fancied a large angled black pipe leading out of the stove, with the washing draped on it to dry.

It was evening when I decided to start. The shops were closed, so it was a question of finding the makings around the house. My family well know me in this mood, which is marked by a general exodous of everyone to the safety of their rooms, together with everything they can carry, for fear I will seize upon it and transform it into dolls' house furniture. However, once my eye fell on the Baby Bio bottle the hunt was over. While trying to decant the contents, however, I decided that the makers are not awfully sporting about the slow exit of their product. At last the bottle was empty and I was surprised to find that there was still some of the evening left. The resulting stove looks very convincing, so to anyone who needs a similar stove I offer the suggestion of how to make it out of a small bottle. Here's the basic idea:

## Materials

*Card*
*Baby Bio bottle*
*Christmas tree light-shade*
*Bracelet links*
*Piece of drinking straw*
*Beads*
*Various fancy bits of broken
   jewellery*
*Black spray paint*

## Method

1 Cut out *Figs i & ii* from card.
2 Score and bend *Fig ii* into box shape.
3 Fit to bottle and glue in place.
4 Glue small and large shelves together to make one.
5 Glue into place on stove top (*Note:* if you can top the shelf with a suitable-sized link, it looks even better).
6 Attach bracelet link as a door.
7 Add handles, name-plate, etc.
8 Spray and paint black, then before the paint dries drag a clean brush over the metal parts to remove some of the paint. This will give a gleam of gold, which looks marvellous and shows up the detail.

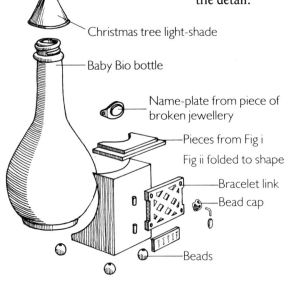

Christmas tree light-shade

Baby Bio bottle

Name-plate from piece of broken jewellery

Pieces from Fig i

Fig ii folded to shape

Bracelet link

Bead cap

Beads

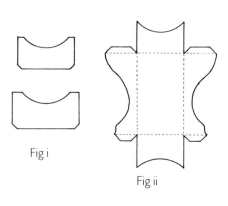

Fig i

Fig ii

# 17

# Chemist

*Ebenezer Cacious was a capable pharmacist with a dream of owning his own dispensary, but he didn't achieve this aim until he met and married Florence when he was in his forties. Flo was a wealthy widow whose husband had been in fish, and her money bought him his much-coveted pharmacy.*

However, Flo did specify that her name should appear on the fascia. A mild man, Ebenezer felt that this was a small price to pay for the shop of his dreams, but explained to her that it would be demeaning for a lady's name to be used in trade! Thus it was decided that her initial only would follow his, and the legend above the shop should read E. F. CACIOUS.

The shop opened in 1896, one year to the day after the wedding, and it was Ebenezer's present to his new wife that at the opening she perceived *her* initial preceding his on the fascia. She was so overwhelmed by his gracious generosity that although she rarely appeared in the shop she loved him for ever. Eb and Flo, as they were affectionately known, soon became pillars of the local community and had a long and happy life together.

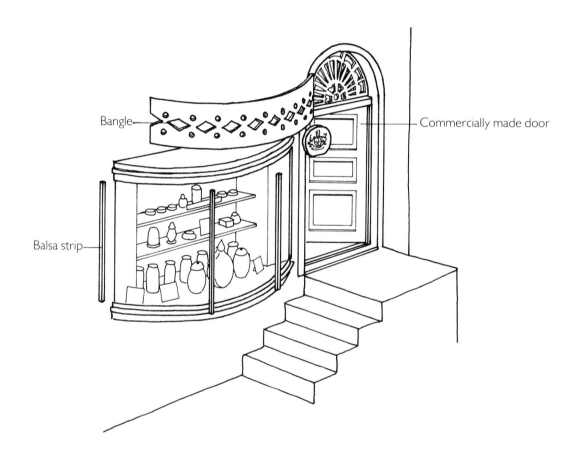

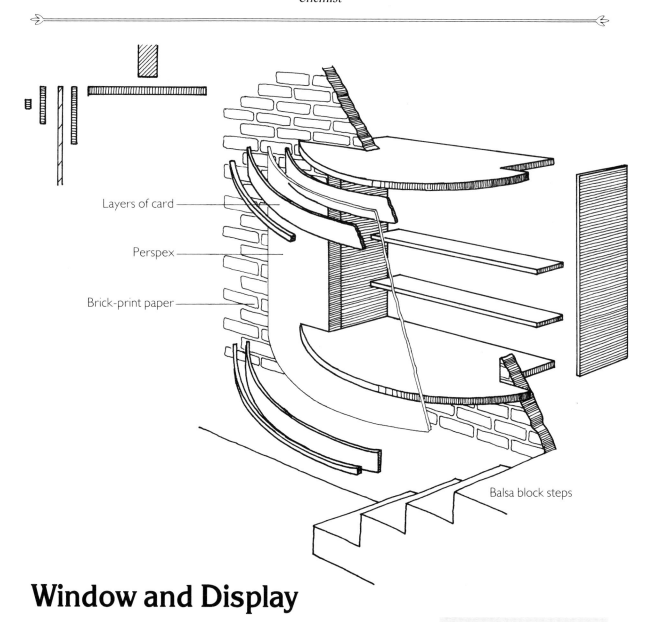

Layers of card

Perspex

Brick-print paper

Balsa block steps

# Window and Display

If I hadn't been able to get my hands on rows of scale bottles and/or jars, I would not have tried to make this kind of shop, but thanks to the nurse who saved me not only ampoules but also their tops (which look like scale milk bottles) and an army friend who kept me supplied with spent cartridges, this problem never arose. (Fountain-pen-ink cartridges make a good substitute, too.)

The bow window itself was built up from layers of card and clear plastic, topped with a railing made from an opened-up bangle. Adverts were cut from reduced photocopies taken from a Victorian magazine. A commercial dolls' house door was set in a frame, using a piece of plastic doyley for the fanlight. Steps were built up from balsa blocks, and brick-print paper finished the job.

To create a suitably fussy and cluttered effect in the window, any of the following can be used.

## Materials

*Small scent-bottle with bead stopper*
*Beads, topped by plastic press-studs*
*Felt-pen tops, with shaft button lids*
*Spent bullet cartridges, topped with metal press-studs*
*Injection ampoules, topped with plastic press-studs*
*Ampoule tops, with insulator cups*
*Cuts from clear drinking-straws*

# Bottles and Jars

If you are contemplating making any shop that contains rows of bottles and jars, think hard as to what materials you can use for the purpose. The problem lies in finding plenty of matching things! Scent phials and trial scent bottles are fine for the odd display bottle in your shop window, but too large for rows. Cutting glass rod is for experts and I failed to master the art, so alternatives were sought and here is a list of possibilities.

## Materials

### Jars and bottles
Cuts from clear plastic tubing
Cuts from clear drinking-straws
Cuts from Biro or Bic pen cases
Doctors' injection ampoules
    and tops
Felt-pen tops
Small cartridges
Faceted glass beads
Poppit beads

### Lids
Small buttons with shaft
    uppermost
Glass or plastic beads
Metal or plastic press-studs
Sequins or card circles from a
    hole punch

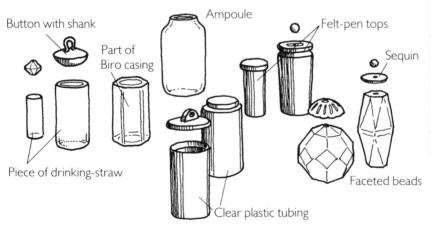

Button with shank
Part of Biro casing
Ampoule
Felt-pen tops
Sequin
Piece of drinking-straw
Clear plastic tubing
Faceted beads

# Sink in Dispensary

Ebenezer does not sell proprietary medicines but prefers to concoct his own remedies, having made his reputation with his personal medicinal compound which is widely believed to cure anything from boils to rust on the automobile. He used to work behind an elaborate screen, but later I removed it because it hid my favourite area around the sink.

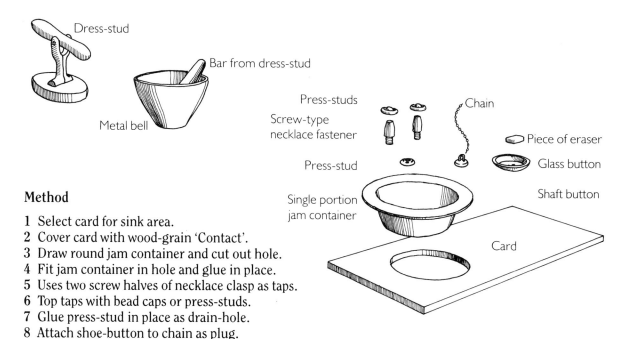

## Method

1 Select card for sink area.
2 Cover card with wood-grain 'Contact'.
3 Draw round jam container and cut out hole.
4 Fit jam container in hole and glue in place.
5 Uses two screw halves of necklace clasp as taps.
6 Top taps with bead caps or press-studs.
7 Glue press-stud in place as drain-hole.
8 Attach shoe-button to chain as plug.
9 Use a glass button for soap-dish and a piece of eraser for soap.

## Materials

### Sink
Card
Wood-grain 'Contact'
Single-portion jam container, perferably oval
Screw-up necklace fasteners
Bead caps
Chain and tiny shoe-button
Press-studs
Glass button for soap-dish
Piece cut from eraser

### Pestle and mortar
The pestle is cut from the bar of a dress-stud
The mortar is a small metal bell

# Scales

Do you remember when 'macho' men sported plated razor-blades on chains around their necks? The fashion has died out now and I for one am delighted because the blades find their way to jumble sales, where I pounce on them to use as stands.

The foot-plate for the larger scale was a link from a chain belt and its embossed surface seemed just right for a stand.

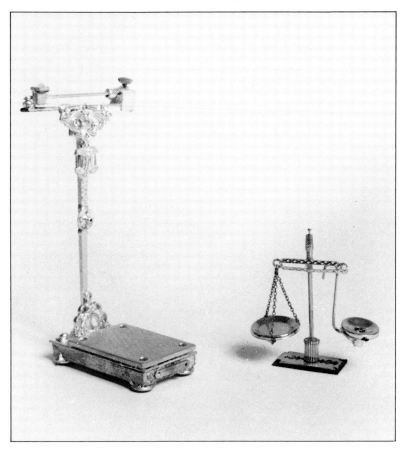

## Method

### Personal weighing scales

 1  Cut balsa-wood base to fit bracelet link; glue link to wood base.
 2  Add two press-studs for feet.
 3  Glue upright tea-stirrer in place.
 4  Back base with slat of wood or half a brooch.
 5  Measure cross-bar (balsa strip) and glue to top of stirrer.
 6  Fit block of balsa, topped with watch-winder, to one end.
 7  Thread bugle bead on to one end of top cross-bar.
 8  Glue block, topped with bead-cap, to other end.
 9  Rest top cross-bar on central bead and glue bead to lower bar.
10  Decorate with broken jewellery.

## Materials

### Personal weighing scales
*Rectangular metal link*
*Balsa wood*
*Macdonalds tea-stirrer*
*Half a brooch frame*
*Metal rod*
*Press-studs*
*Necklace clasp*
*Beads*
*Watch-winder*
*Jewellery bits*

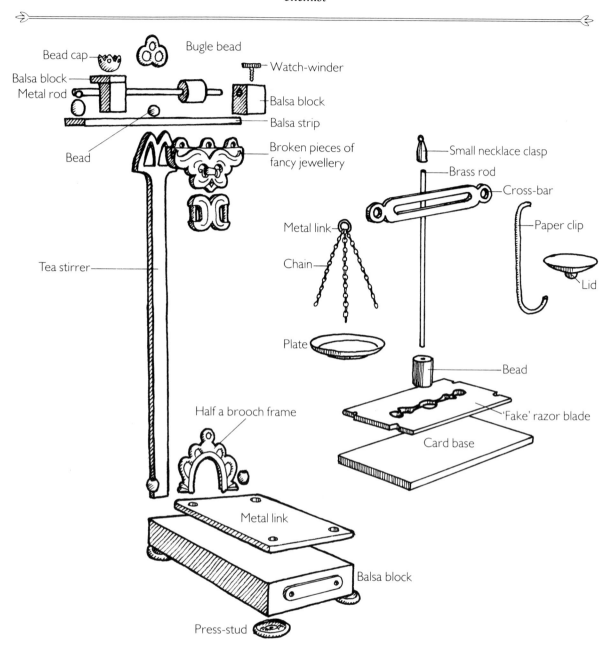

Bead cap

Bugle bead

Balsa block

Metal rod

Watch-winder

Balsa block

Balsa strip

Bead

Broken pieces of fancy jewellery

Small necklace clasp

Brass rod

Cross-bar

Metal link

Paper clip

Chain

Lid

Tea stirrer

Plate

Bead

'Fake' razor blade

Half a brooch frame

Card base

Metal link

Balsa block

Press-stud

**Beam scales**

*Plated razor-blade or half
  a hinge*
*Screw necklace clasp*
*Bead*
*Brass rod*
*Metal link and tiny chain*
*Plate and lid from dolls' house
  tea set*
*Paper clip*

Beam scales

The cross-bar of this was found, and I don't know what it is, so I'll just refer to it as a bar.

1  Cut card base to fit your razor-blade; glue.
2  Mount necklace clasp or bead in centre of blade; glue.
3  Top brass rod with half a small necklace clasp.
4  Glue rod upright on to bead or clasp.
5  Place cross-bar in position.
6  Glue three pieces of chain to plate; gather loose ends into a link.
7  Fix to bar at one end.
8  Open up paper clip and cut off S-shape. Use this to hang lid from other end of bar.

# Chair

I have to admit that chairs are not my strong point. However, I made this one from a frame cut in card and, finding some jolly little turned cocktail sticks, used two as uprights to support a brooch as the back-rest.

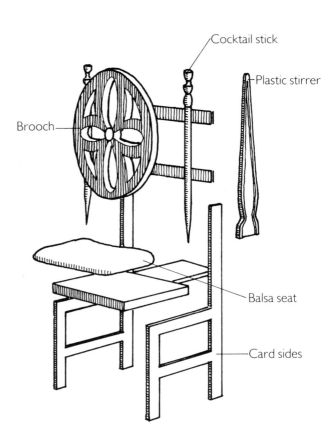

Cocktail stick

Plastic stirrer

Brooch

Balsa seat

Card sides

## Method

1 Cut two sides from firm card.
2 Cut two chair seats from balsa wood – seat to be the same width as brooch.
3 Paint one seat red (for cushion).
4 Glue seat and brooch between sides.
5 Decorate uprights with cocktail sticks and/or plastic stirrer.

## Materials

*Card*
*Balsa wood*
*Plastic stirrer*
*Cocktail sticks*
*Brooches*

# 18

# Photographer

*Charles Vernon Birdie, from a distinguished family who reside in Pray Manor – you must have heard of the Birdies of Pray – was the first of his family to go into trade. He rather disappointed his father, who had expected him to go into the church – only I can't make churches, so he didn't! However, as photography was reasonably genteel, and artistic rather than remunerative, he was forgiven and not thrown out of the nest.*

# Exterior

If making a shop in a hurry, I suggest you work out the size of the box you need and take the measurements to your DIY dealer, who will supply the wood and cut it to size. Look out for stick-on mouldings while you are there.

The front of my shop lifts off and I then attach it to the shop proper using bar magnets. I've used Foamcore (*see* Useful Materials) to make the shop façade and the inside arch. For speed, I allowed myself to incorporate a commercial door and window, merely setting them into the Foamcore.

## Materials

*1 piece 10" × 13" 6mm ply (for base)*
*1 piece 9" × 13" 4mm ply (for back)*
*2 pieces 9" × 9" 4mm ply (for sides)*
*1 dolls' house door*
*1 dolls' house Georgian window*
*Brick-paper and stick-on mouldings*
*Strip wood beading*

*Shop dimensions = 13" × 10½" × 9"*

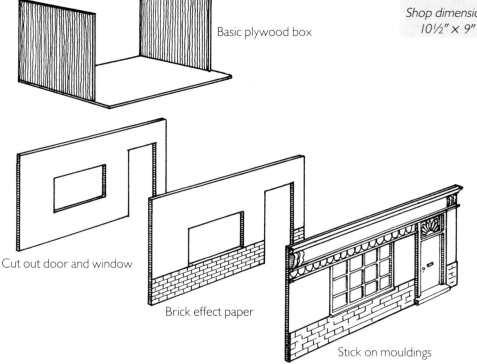

Basic plywood box

Cut out door and window

Brick effect paper

Stick on mouldings

## Method

1　Assemble box, allowing slight sill on the floor to protrude.
2　Try front piece for size and make sure it is large enough.
3　Cut spaces for door (leaving fanlight) and window; glue them in place.
4　Cut strip of card; cover in brick-paper. Glue in place below window.
5　Build up fascia using wood beading and moulding.
6　Add lettering (I use dry print). Print on to a separate piece of paper (to be added later) to allow for mistakes.

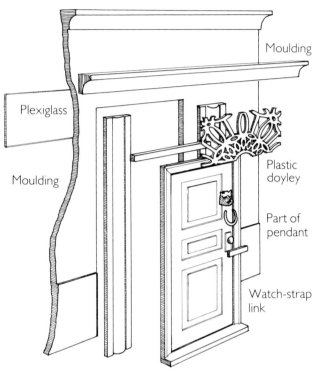

Moulding

Plexiglass

Moulding

Plastic doyley

Part of pendant

Watch-strap link

# Doorway

In other shops (see Arthur Tick) I have made my own doors, building them up from layers of card and decorating them with bracelet links, but for this shop I used a commercial dolls' house door and simply added the detail. The fanlight bars were made from a plastic doyley. Years ago I was lucky to find a pendant decorated with three lion's heads which I have been saving to make into knockers. Once found, it was just a question of adding part of a chain-link as a bar to it and gluing. However, if you can't find a lion's head, an earring or dress-stud would do just as well. The letterbox was one link from a 'gold' watch-strap.

## Method

1  Cut door-space, allowing for fanlight as well as door.
2  Fit commercial door.
3  Glue Plexiglass across back of fanlight space.
4  Attach fanlight bars, cut from centre of doyley.
5  Glue on link as a letterbox.
6  Make knocker out of suitable object and attach ¾ link as knocker bar.

## Materials

*Plastic doyley*
*Lion's head, earring or stud*
*Watch-strap link*
*Balsa-wood strip*
*Plexiglass*

# Window Display

In this instance I used a commercial window and set it in the front wall. The photographs and prices can always be photocopied if you are reluctant to spoil magazines or books. Don't forget that photocopiers can reduce pictures to the size you require: very useful!

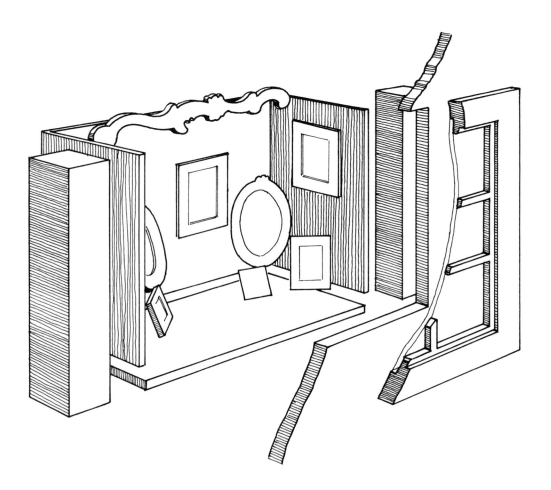

## Method

1 Flank back of window with ½″ balsa-wood strip.
2 Score and bend card to form window depth and display area.
3 Fit this 'box' with a card floor.
4 Glue decorative strip to box top and trim card to fit.
5 Build up display of goods; dress window before you stick it in place.
6 Glue behind window.

## Materials

*Dolls' house window and*
*    Plexiglass*
*Card and balsa-wood strip*
*Small photographs and prices*
*Earrings, brooches, links for*
*    frames*
*Plastic moulding strip*

# Interior

I have always respected books and rarely abuse them, but from the moment I owned a reproduction of a Victorian lady's scrapbook I knew that I was going to cut chunks out of it. It was full of sepia photographs and there were a few small, prissy watercolours done by the lady. Though some of the photographs would be too large to use, often the background people were small enough. What to make of them? A photographer's, of course!

I used the lady's watercolours as a series of backdrops for the sitters and a menu's edging as the trim for an arch. Circular links from a chain belt made some of the picture frames; larger photographs were framed in metal 35mm slide mounts, which I made more elaborate by gluing bead caps and bits of jewellery on to them. Wood-grain Contact was used to give a panelled effect to the walls. The cupboards in the rear were made in card, letting in bracelet links for detail, then sprayed brown to give an all-over effect.

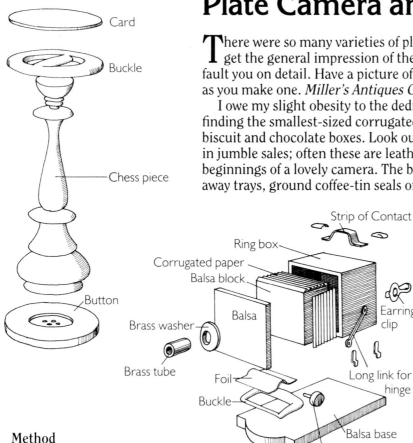

Card

Buckle

Chess piece

Button

# Plate Camera and Stand

There were so many varieties of plate camera that provided you get the general impression of them only an expert is likely to fault you on detail. Have a picture of the real thing in front of you as you make one. *Miller's Antiques Guide* is a good reference.

I owe my slight obesity to the dedicated research that went to finding the smallest-sized corrugated paper, located only in biscuit and chocolate boxes. Look out for ring or other small boxes in jumble sales; often these are leather-covered and make the beginnings of a lovely camera. The brass shim I get from take-away trays, ground coffee-tin seals or metal throw-away ashtrays.

Strip of Contact

Ring box

Corrugated paper

Balsa block

Balsa

Brass washer

Earring clip

Brass tube

Foil

Long link for hinge

Buckle

Balsa base

Winder

## Method

### Camera

1 Find or make small box; cut balsa block to fit loosely into it.
2 Cover top and both sides of balsa block with corrugated paper.
3 Cut front for camera; glue in place.
4 Glue brass washer in centre front and fit tube into it.
5 Cover larger box with the Contact.
6 Cut base that will allow room for camera, box and buckle.
7 Glue box and camera into place on base.
8 Glue buckle on to front of base.
9 Add winder, inserted into a foil setting.
10 Use hinge and stick in place.
11 Add carrying handle cut from thin strip of brown Contact.
12 Add brass side catch (earring-clip), brass ends to carrying handle and box strengtheners.

### Stand

1 Cut off bishop's head (half-way down, between his nose and his mouth, if he had one).
2 Mount him on a large button for a base.
3 Fill in centre of buckle with card.
4 Glue buckle to bishop's head for a table.
5 Spray brown.

## Materials

### Camera
Ring box, 1½″ × 1¼″ × ¾″ approx.
Balsa-wood pieces
Small-scale corrugated paper
Brass tube
Brass washer
Watch-strap buckle
Watch-winder
Brown wood-grain Contact
Brass-coloured foil
Earring clasp
Long link

### Stand
Chess piece (bishop, king, queen or castle)
Button for base

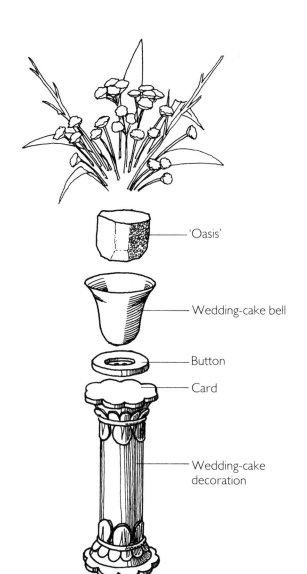

'Oasis'

Wedding-cake bell

Button

Card

Wedding-cake
decoration

# Flower Arrangement

I was going to sit a baby on a pillar, but a flower arrangement looked more decorative so that's what I ended up making. Next time you go to a wedding, refuse the cake – it will only make you fat – and instead go for the decorations. You can make no end of things from them!

## Materials

*Wedding-cake pillar*
*Circle of cardboard*
*Wedding-cake bell*
*Fancy button or brooch minus*
  *stone*
*Dried flowers and Oasis*

### Method

1  Cement base of bell to button to make an urn.
2  Force a small chunk of Oasis into bell.
3  Arrange sprigs of tiny dried flowers, gluing as you go.
4  Cut circle to fit top of column. Glue in place.

# Bench

You can often pick up rectangular boxes in jumble sales; if they are jewellery boxes they may even have a leatherette finish, saving you the job of covering them. If not, it's a matter of moments to cover with material.

## Materials

*Rectangular box (jewellery, cycle puncture outfit box or similar)*
*Lampshade gimp or brocade edging*
*Two bracelet links or small buckles*

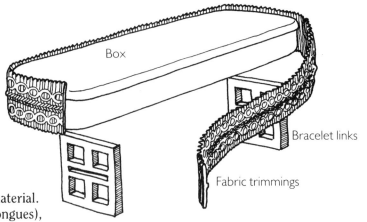

Box

Bracelet links

Fabric trimmings

## Method

1  Cover box with fabric if necessary.
2  Glue edging to cover raw ends of material.
3  Add legs made of buckles (minus tongues), or bracelet links.

# FURTHER INFORMATION

# Making Dolls

*There are many ways you can go about making dolls.
Mine need to be flexible as I want to pose them, and it
is important that their hands be able to grasp things,
so I have evolved my own way of making them. For
male figures, no sewing is required!*

## Materials

*Pipe cleaners*
*Beads*
*Cotton wool, nylon hair or*
    *embroidery cotton*
*Paint*
*Polyfilla*

### Male

*Felt*
*Fine fabric*
*Cardboard*
*Paper*

## Method

1 The basic body shape is made from pipe cleaners, with the arms left long enough to make hands which will grasp.
2 The head is a bead, but always make the body and dress it before attaching the head.
3 Hair and whiskers are cotton wool, cotton or nylon hair, glued to the head.
4 Polyfilla can be used to build up faces and establish character, especially in male figures.
5 Features are drawn or painted on.

## Male

1 Establish the character by creating the hair style, whiskers, etc.
2 Begin dressing with the boots, made from felt, and cardboard soles. Figures are sometimes difficult to stand up, so make the feet over-sized, and if they will still not stand by themselves, put a blob of Blu-tack under each sole.
3 For the trousers, measure the leg to the waist and cut two strips of suitable material. Fold and stick, with the join inside the leg, one leg at a time.
4 I usually make the dicky from white paper.
5 Cut the jacket from matching material.
6 Make the lapels from black paper.
7 Finally, attach the head.

Bead built up with Polyfilla

Pipe cleaners

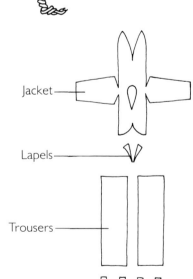

Jacket

Lapels

Trousers

Felt boots

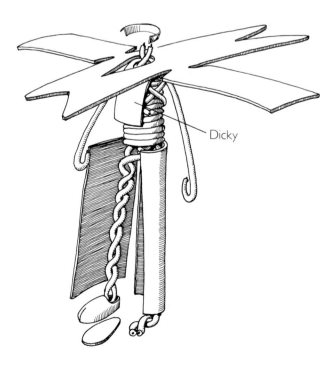

Dicky

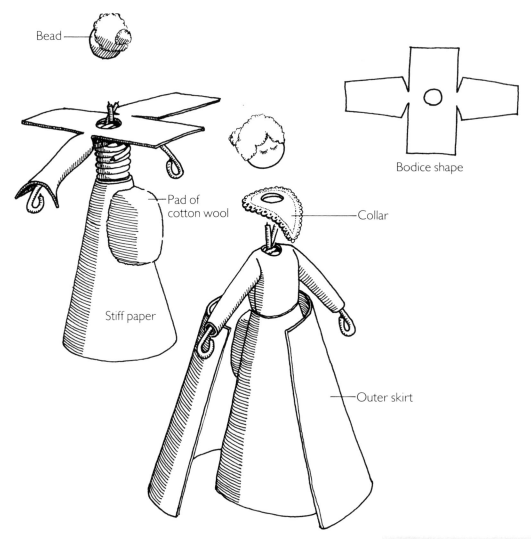

Bead

Pad of cotton wool

Stiff paper

Bodice shape

Collar

Outer skirt

### Female

1 Pile the cotton wool (or alternative) on wet glue on the bead head and tease out into a long strand. Twist the strand into a hair style. Do not add the head until last.

2 Make the basic female shape by gluing a pad of cotton wool to the back of the underskirt, which is made from stiff paper. Dress the lower half of the body.

3 Cut out the bodice shape as shown and dress the upper half of the body.

4 Cut the outer skirt from suitable fabric and stick over the underskirt.

5 Add the cuffs and collar, and any other detail.

6 The mob cap is a circle, gathered and trimmed, and stuck to the hair.

7 Use bits of ribbon, lace and tiny buttons to create various characters and effects.

8 Last of all, fix the head in position.

*Female*
*Stiff paper*
*Fine fabric*
*Lace, narrow ribbon, tiny buttons etc.*

# 20

# What Can I Make From These?

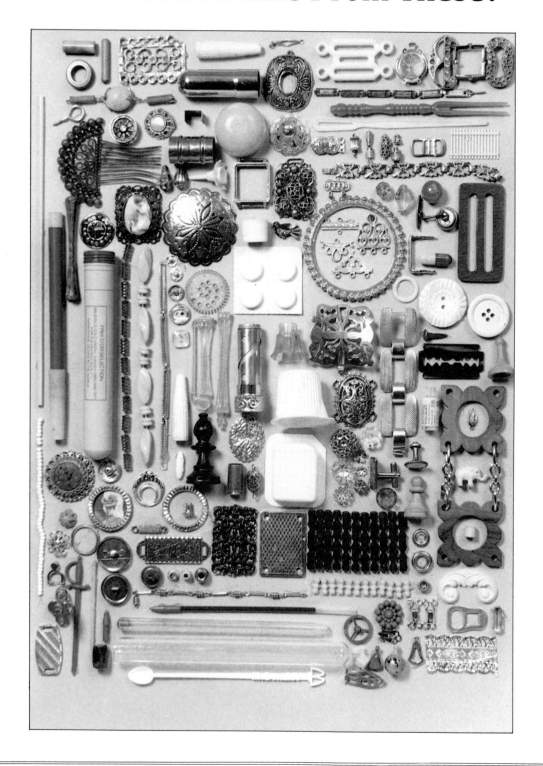

# Finding Materials

While it is good to be constantly on the look-out for useful modelling materials (and you can find them in the most unexpected places), I must admit my behaviour can become a bit obsessive. I once embarrassed my husband by removing a large square of a textured paper tablecloth laid over a grubby linen cloth at a café in Brittany, as I could see it would make a perfect Victorian ceiling. I was anxious to take a piece of it before it got covered in food! Faced with a large square hole where my place setting should have been, the waiter gaped, cutlery in hand, while I found myself launching into an explanation, in schoolgirl French, about how it is the custom in England to take home the paper mat you have dined on to show your friends. He then rallied and rose to great heights of gallantry by presenting me with a whole (unsullied) paper tablecloth, and has probably bewildered successive English diners ever since by sending off each of them clutching a paper cloth! The ceilings looked very authentic, though.

However, the point I hope I have made is that almost *anything* can be pressed into service, provided you keep an open mind and use plenty of imagination. Remember, this book is to give ideas and inspiration, rather than lay down hard and fast rules, and the things to look for are shapes and textures and so forth (like the tablecloth above!) which suggest other objects, and which inspire you to try to make them.

Look out for broken jewellery, embossed cake-strip, corrugated paper, single-portion cream, jam, milk and butter dishes, plastic shampoo nozzles, toothpaste and felt-pen tops, plastic preformed pill packs, clear plastic bubble-packs, buckles, beads and bead caps, buttons (with or without shafts), metal or plastic cigar tubes, test tubes, wheels, cartridges, drinking-straws, lipstick cases, ring-pulls, chess pieces, small bells, metal bracelet links, necklace clasps, paper clips and fasteners, pins and map-pins, dress-studs and cuff-links, charms, watch parts, pill capsules, ampoules, rods, toothpicks and cocktail sticks, Bic and Biro pens.

# 21

# Tools, Methods and Materials

My whole approach to modelling is that of someone who has little expertise with tools, but several suspicious males in the house who prise any I may have 'borrowed' out of my hand. Thus I have developed both a furtive look and a small collection of my own tools. Howls of derision greeted my announcement that I was about to advise others on this subject, so I won't – except to say that I've taken to the glue-gun and now that I've found this marvellous way of gluing I'm sticking to it!

It is my proud boast that I have made everything in my dolls' house and shops and I keep costs to the minimum.

My method of embellishing plain objects with stuck-on twiddly-bits does rely on uniting the disparate parts with a good paint job when the object is complete, and nothing does this so well as the cellulose paint spray sold in cans for automobile repairs. There is plenty of colour choice and a fine spray which gets into – but doesn't clutter – even the smallest details. It dries fast and covers well, leaving the cardboard strengthened and waterproofed, but remember that *it must be used in the open air.* For paint jobs where spray is not suitable, use watercolour and then varnish it; it will even adhere to shiny surfaces if you drag your brush across a bar of toilet soap before mixing the colour.

# My Choice of Tools

Drawing-board; Glue-gun; Modeller's scalpel; Steel ruler; Modeller's saw; Pliers; Files; Glass-cutter; Leather punch; Scissors.

# Some Useful Materials

### DIY

Plywood – use 6mm for bases, 4mm for walls
Copydex – for the few occasions where the glue-gun doesn't serve
Wooden beading
Stick-on moulding
Balsa-wood bundles – give you a variety of assorted pieces
Bar magnets – now available in strip form; cut where you like
Spray paint
Fymo – brilliantly coloured modelling material which hardens in minutes in the oven

### Art Shops

Foamcore – a useful non-warp board, usually sold for mounting
   board, available in sheets 20″ × 30″ and larger
Dry-print lettering, available in a wide variety of types and sizes,
   useful if your own lettering is dodgy
Manila card

### Stationers

Be on the lookout for gift-wrap papers to use as wallpapers or for floors, also for motifs.

Hobbies and Models Ltd stock almost all dolls'-house and modellers' needs, and will mail your order. Their address is 217 Streatfield Road, Harrow, Middlesex (tel: 081–204–9867).

# Bibliography

*Furnishing Dolls' Houses.* Audrey Johnson, Bell & Hyman.
*Book of Miniatures.* Helen Ruthberg, Chilton Press,

# Reference

*Antique Household Gadgets and Appliances.* David de Haan,
  Blandford Press.
*Edwardian Shopping (A selection from the Army and Navy
  Catalogues 1896–1913).* David and Charles.
*Miller's Antiques Price Guide.*

Patricia King was born – yes! – and educated at an astonishing variety of schools, both state and private, progressive and boarding, and then at art school. She has worked as a display artist and window dresser, in an advertising art studio and as a teacher. After living in the USA for three years, she now teaches pottery and crafts to nursery nurses at two colleges of further education. She can't resist making anything in the craft line that can be made!

Married with three children, and a nice variety of grandchildren, she writes and illustrates stories and has done a little broadcasting (Woman's Hour, not the Reith Lectures!). Amongst other things, she arranges displays for pottery and crafts exhibitions and gets dragged into painting huge backgrounds for local amateur dramatics societies. When exhibiting at crafts fairs the dolls' house furniture she has made, she has to explain that it is not for sale – she is just there to show people how to make it.

Patricia King can be heard shrieking to students, family, friends and anyone who will listen: 'Don't buy it, you can make it!'

OTHER TITLES AVAILABLE FROM

# GMC Publications Ltd

### BOOKS

| | |
|---|---|
| Woodworking Plans and Projects | GMC Publications |
| 40 More Woodworking Plans and Projects | GMC Publications |
| Woodworking Crafts Annual | GMC Publications |
| Turning Miniatures in Wood | John Sainsbury |
| Woodcarving: A Complete Course | Ron Butterfield |
| Pleasure and Profit from Woodturning | Reg Sherwin |
| Making Unusual Miniatures | Graham Spalding |
| Furniture Projects for the Home | Ernest Parrott |
| Seat Weaving | Ricky Holdstock |
| Green Woodwork | Mike Abbott |
| The Incredible Router | Jeremy Broun |
| Electric Woodwork | Jeremy Broun |
| Woodturning: A Foundation Course | Keith Rowley |
| Upholstery: A Complete Course | David James |
| Making Shaker Furniture | Barry Jackson |
| Making Tudor Dolls' Houses | Derek Rowbottom |
| Making Georgian Dolls' Houses | Derek Rowbottom |
| Making Period Dolls' House Furniture | Derek & Sheila Rowbottom |
| Heraldic Miniature Knights | Peter Greenhill |
| Furniture Projects | Rod Wales |
| Restoring Rocking Horses | Clive Green & Anthony Dew |
| Making Fine Furniture: Projects | Tom Darby |
| Making & Modifying Woodworking Tools | Jim Kingshott |
| Multi-Centre Woodturning | Ray Hopper |
| Woodturning Wizardry | David Springett |
| Complete Woodfinishing | Ian Hosker |
| Little Boxes from Wood | John Bennett |
| Members' Guide to Marketing | Jack Pigden |
| Woodworkers' Career & Educational Source Book | GMC Publications |

GMC Publications regularly produces new books on a wide range of woodworking and craft
subjects, and an increasing number of specialist magazines, all available on subscription:

### MAGAZINES

FURNITURE    WOODCARVING    WOODTURNING    BUSINESSMATTERS

All these books and magazines are available through bookshops and newsagents, or may be ordered
by post from the publishers at 166 High Street, Lewes, East Sussex BN7 1XU, telephone (0273)
477374. Credit card orders are accepted. Please write or phone for the latest information.